DEDICATION

To Pam Thomas:

Your joyous spirit and dedication are so very appreciated.
Thank you for everything you do to ensure the smooth running of
our day-to-day operations and for being such a good friend.

Series Created By • Beverly Cohn
Designers • Peter Hess & Marguerite Jones
Research • Laurie Cohn

Special thanks to Kenny Bookbinder for his invaluable help with the Sports section.

CONTENTS

POLITICS

& WORLD EVENTS

EISENHOWER BECOMES PRESIDENT

Soldier-statesman **Dwight D. Eisenhower** takes the oath of office as the nation's 34th president. The popular general is the first Republican president in 20 years and first soldier-president since Ulysses S. Grant held office in 1869.

President Eisenhower receives good wishes from his predecessor, Harry S. Truman.

The new Chief Executive takes the reins of government during a climactic moment in the country's history when the solutions of foreign and domestic problems press for early decisions. He pledges to faithfully serve America and says he will *"neither compromise, nor tire, nor ever cease"* in seeking honorable world peace.

1953

United States

Harry S. Truman

Mrs. Clare Boothe Luce takes office as U.S. ambassador to Italy.

Robert F. Wagner, Jr. elected mayor of New York—**Robert B. Meyner** new governor of New Jersey.

Harry S. Truman leaves the presidency with a 31% approval rating according to the latest Gallup poll.

Robert Taft elected U.S. Senate Republican leader.

SENATOR TAFT DIES

Known as "Mr. Republican" and one of the nation's most respected leaders, death comes to Robert A. Taft. His passing is mourned by all political groups.

Joseph McCarthy

Despite **Senator McCarthy's** opposition, **Charles Bohlen** named U.S. ambassador to U.S.S.R.

Accused of aiding Communists by **Senator Joseph McCarthy**, former President Truman refuses to testify before House Un-American Activities Committee after receiving subpoena.

Dwight D. Eisenhower

President Eisenhower meets with West German Chancellor **Konrad Adenauer** in Washington.

President Eisenhower proposes "Atoms for Peace" international energy stockpile.

WHAT A YEAR IT WAS!

Adlai Stevenson Speech

In New York, **Adlai Stevenson**, defeated presidential candidate, makes his first major post-campaign speech at the Democrats' Jefferson-Jackson Day dinner.

On hand are **Eleanor Roosevelt** and **Sam Rayburn** *(top)*, **Senator Herbert Lehman** and **New York's Mayor Vincent Impellitteri** *(center)* and Stevenson's running mate, **Senator John Sparkman**, and **Margaret Truman** *(bottom)*.

An ovation greets the party's titular leader, who urges that the Eisenhower administration be given a fair chance to prove itself.

"The Republican Party is attempting what has not been tried for a long time—government by businessmen. America has always been a nation ripe for experiment. We Democrats have experimented boldly and accomplished miracles."

1953 KOREAN WAR

In Korea,

three years of combat ends as United Nations and Communist negotiators meet at Panmunjom on July 27th to sign an armistice.

Syngman Rhee

While South Korea boycotts the signing ceremony, President Syngman Rhee reluctantly agrees to observe the armistice for a limited time, awaiting settlement on Korea's new border and return of POWs.

The long war undertaken to stop Red aggression is over with the enemy holding less territory than before. The cost has been bitter for both sides: almost 25,000 American soldiers killed and more than 100,000 injured; over one million South Koreans killed and millions homeless; more than one million Communists dead.

WHAT A YEAR IT WAS!

ENDS

With fighting ended, a political conference is slated to deal with the touchy problem of unifying Korea and assuring peace.

Neutral observers are already present to oversee adherence to armistice terms.

President Eisenhower addresses the nation.

*"**W**e have won an armistice on a single battleground—not peace in the world. We may not now relax our guard nor cease our quest. Throughout the coming months, during the period of prisoner screening and exchange and during the possibly longer period of the political conference, which looks toward the unification of Korea, we and our United Nations allies must be vigilant against the possibility of untoward developments."*

WHAT A YEAR IT WAS!

A PIPE DREAM COMES TRUE

Now millions more feet of Orangeburg Pipe to fill the demand

WEST COAST PLANT
NEWARK, CALIFORNIA

HOME PLANT
ORANGEBURG, NEW YORK

A new Orangeburg plant on the Pacific Coast and extensive expansions of the home plant at Orangeburg, N. Y., are now striving to meet the nation's demand for modern root-proof pipe.

This demand for home, farm, and industry, led by plumbers who know pipe values, is overwhelming. And the reason is plain —only Orangeburg, the modern root-proof pipe, offers so many superior features.

TAP...TAP...TAP...
and you have an easily assembled, leak-proof joint without need of cement, compounds, swabbing, or reaming. And Orangeburg is light! A man easily carries several lengths at once. These and its many other advantages have helped to make Orangeburg America's most-wanted pipe.

ROOTS CAN'T DRINK HERE!
A pipeline with leaky joints attracts roots... but Orangeburg pipelines have watertight Taperweld® Joints that keep out roots. Pipe, joints, and fittings form an impenetrable barrier against root entry and clogging.

Look for the Name

ORANGEBURG
Root-Proof Pipe

Make sure you get *genuine* Orangeburg Root-Proof Pipe for house-sewer or septic tank connections, for storm drains and other non-pressure uses outside the home. Use the *Perforated* for septic tank beds, foundation drains, wet spots in lawns and fields. Write Dept. SE93 for more facts about Orangeburg pipe and fittings.
ORANGEBURG MANUFACTURING CO., INC., ORANGEBURG, N.Y.

41 YEARS UNDERGROUND AND GOOD AS NEW.
Yes, twice the time Rip Van Winkle enjoyed his nap, yet it is good for many more years of good service. It's tough, strong, resilient material —withstands traffic shocks and soil settlements .... and also resists the acids and alkalies found in ground waters and sewage wastes.

10

ASIA

- A Settlement Is Reached By Korean Truce Negotiators On Exchange Of Sick And Wounded Prisoners.

- In Protest Over Armistice Terms, Seoul Threatens To Remove Army From U.N. Rule.

- U.N. Truce Banned By South Korean Representatives.

- South Korean President **Rhee** Rebuked By **Eisenhower** For Releasing North Korean Prisoners Against Will Of U.N.

- Under Terms Of Korean Armistice Communists Free First 400 U.N. Prisoners.

- Mutual Defense Pact Signed In Seoul By American Secretary Of State John Foster Dulles And South Korean Foreign Minister Pyun Yung Tai.

- One British And 23 American POWs Refuse Repatriation And Remain With Their North Korean Communist Captors.

- U.S. General **Mark Clark** Supports Use Of A-Bomb If Koreans Violate Truce.

- Two U.S. Divisions Slated To Withdraw From Korea.

Ramon Magsaysay Is New Filipino President.

- On A Vote Of No Confidence By The House Of Representatives, Government Of Japanese Premier **Shigeru Yoshida** Is Ousted.

- 10-Year Treaty Of Friendship, Commerce And Navigation Signed By U.S. And Japan.

- While Patrolling Formosa Straight, U.S. Navy Bomber Shot Down By Anti-Aircraft Fire.

- Paving The Way For The Nationalists To Attack Communists, Ike Announces He Will Pull Out Seventh Fleet From Formosa.

- Seven Killed And Five Wounded On British Launch When Chinese Communist Warship Opens Fire.

- Chinese Communist Pilot Surrenders To U.S. After Landing MiG-15 Near Seoul.

Ending Six-Day Exile In Thailand, Cambodian King **Sihanouk** Returns To Bangkok.

1953 ★ Indochina

China
Vietnam
Laos
Cambodia

War Factories Hidden In Jungle By Viet Minh Destroyed By French Forces.

France Offered Increased Aid In Vietnam By President Eisenhower.

40,000 Viet Minh Troops Invade Laos.

French-Led Forces Evacuate Northern Laos.

In Laos, Viet Minh Retreat With Onset Of Monsoon Season.

To Support French Effort In Vietnam, Eisenhower Authorizes $60 Million In Military Aid.

U.S. Warns France Of Domino Effect In Southeast Asia – General Henri Eugene Navarre Appointed New Commander-In-Chief Of French Union Forces In Indochina.

Laos And Vietnam Agree To French Talks On Independence.

"Operation Seagull" Begins In Tonkin Delta By French Union Troops.

In Surprise Attack Against The Viet Minh, French Paratroopers Launch "Operation Castor," Capturing A Strategic Plateau, Dien Bien Phu.

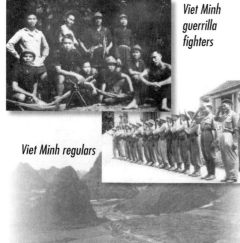

Viet Minh guerrilla fighters

Viet Minh regulars

EUROPE

The Dutch Government Announces That No U.S. Aid Is Needed By The Netherlands.

Great Britain Sends Troops To British Guiana To Prevent Communist Rebellion.

De Gaulle

European Defense Community Condemned By France's General Charles De Gaulle.

In Paris, France Signs Pact Granting Laos Independence Within French Union.

Seeking An End To Air Clashes, The Big Four Meet In Berlin For First Time In Two Years.

In East Berlin, Soviet Tanks Crush Uprising By Thousands Of Workers, Which Begins As Protest Against Increased Construction Quotas But Escalates Into National Strike.

West German Chancellor Adenauer Appoints Former Nazi To Cabinet.

Greece, Turkey And Yugoslavia Sign 5-Year Defense Pact.

In Exchange For Economic And Military Aid, Agreement Is Reached Between Spain And The U.S. Allowing Construction Of American Military Bases On Spanish Soil.

In Major Reshuffle Of Government Posts, Imre Nagy Replaces Mátyás Rákosi As Premier Of Hungary — Declares Intentions To Cultivate Trade Relations With Capitalist As Well As Communist Countries.

The Big 3 — **U.S.** (President Eisenhower), **Great Britain** (Prime Minister Sir Winston Churchill) And **France** (Premier Joseph Laniel) — Meet In Bermuda Reaffirming Their Unity Under NATO.

WHAT A YEAR IT WAS!

Political parties in Italy go all out to entice citizens to the polls.

Italian Election

The two-day election sees the parties of the leftist Communists and rightist Monarchists align against the four-party pro-western coalition group, headed by Italy's present premier, Alcide de Gasperi.

There are over 8,300 candidates for a new Senate and Chamber of Deputies and the voters are confused.

Every precaution is taken to assure a quiet election.

De Gasperi, premier since 1945, loses election to Guiseppe Pella and resigns.

The Soviet

Joseph Stalin, the most powerful dictator in Russian history, dies of a brain hemorrhage in Moscow, dealing world Communism a heavy blow and opening a struggle for power among leaders in the Kremlin.

A panel headed by Nikita Khrushchev, secretary of the Communist Party's Central Committee, makes the funeral arrangements and Stalin's body is entombed beside that of Lenin.

In what is considered one of the most remarkable stories in history, Stalin will be remembered for his ruthlessness, tyrannical power and shrewd diplomatic maneuvering, masterminding the transition from ally of the West in a hot war to enemy in the cold war. A brilliant military commander, under his leadership the Soviets were the first to beat Hitler.

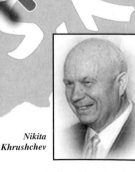

Nikita Khrushchev

Georgi **Malenkov** Named Soviet Premier Upon **Stalin's** Death.

Nikita **Khrushchev** Replaces **Georgi Malenkov** As Secretary Of Communist Party.

Soviet First Deputy Premier **Lavrenti Beria** Is Fired, Charged With Lusting For Power And Trying To Introduce Capitalism Into The Soviet Union.

Former Soviet Deputy Premier **Lavrenti Beria** And Six Of His Aides Shot To Death By Firing Squad For Conspiring Against The Communist Party And Attempting To Restore A Capitalist State.

Union

Confirming That The U.S. Has Developed The H-Bomb, President Truman Warns Stalin, In His Last State Of The Union Address, That War Would Mean Ruin For The U.S.S.R.

The U.S.S.R. And The U.S. Can Resolve Their Differences Through Peaceful Negotiations, Asserts Soviet Premier G. M. Malenkov In His Inaugural Address To The Supreme Soviet.

Soviet Premier Georgi Malenkov Announces Development Of The Hydrogen Bomb, Ending U.S. Monopoly On This Powerful Weapon.

U.S. troops witness a plume of radioactive smoke rise after a test blast at Yucca Flats, Nevada.

The Soviet Union Vetoes Nomination Of Canadian **Lester B. Pearson** As U.N. Secretary General. The Security Council Recommends 47-Year-Old Swedish Minister Of State **Dag Hammarskjöld** To Succeed **Trygve Lie**.

Dag Hammarskjöld

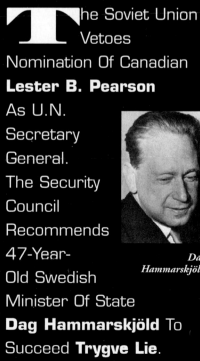

WHAT A YEAR IT WAS!

1953

THE COLD WAR

TRIESTE

- 🌐 Yugoslavia's President Tito Ready To Support NATO To Keep Peace.

- 🌐 Leaving Allied Occupation Zone A To Italy, U.S. And Britain Pull Out Of Trieste.

- 🌐 President Tito Threatens Attack If Italy Enters Zone A.

- 🌐 Italian Premier Pella Threatens Resignation If U.S. And Great Britain Yield To Yugoslavia On Trieste.

- 🌐 U.S. And British Troops Dispatched To Trieste Due To Widespread Rioting.

- 🌐 Italy And Yugoslavia Agree To Withdraw Forces From Trieste Border Area.

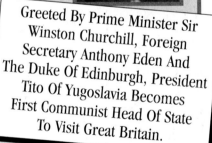

Yugoslavia's Marshal Tito

Greeted By Prime Minister Sir Winston Churchill, Foreign Secretary Anthony Eden And The Duke Of Edinburgh, President Tito Of Yugoslavia Becomes First Communist Head Of State To Visit Great Britain.

✈ British 4-Engine Bomber Shot Down By Soviets In Berlin-Hamburg Air Corridor.

✈ Political Asylum And $50,000 Offered To Communist Pilots By U.S. For Delivery Of MiG Jet.

★ Ike Offers $15 Million In Aid To East Berlin If Kremlin Agrees.

🔫 200 U.N. Soldiers Including 64 Americans Are Released From Communist Korean Captivity.

🔫 Over 7,000 Political Prisoners Receive Amnesty From Yugoslavian Government.

★ In Big Four Talks Proposed By The West, Soviets Demand Peking Delegate Be Included.

Relying Heavily On Nuclear Weapons, NATO Ends 11th Session In Accord On Long-Range Arms Plan.

WHAT A YEAR IT WAS!

"Fresh up" with Seven-Up!

Copyright 1953 by The Seven-Up Company

Get a family supply of 24 bottles. *Buy 7-Up by the case. Or get the handy* 7-Up Family Pack. *Easy-lift center handle, easy to store.*

The All-Family Drink!
You like it...it likes you!

With the pyramids built and Gaul divided into three parts, nothing is so pleasant a reminder of the present, no *reward* for good work so *good* . . . as sparkling, crystal-clear 7-Up! What's more, 7-Up is so pure, so wholesome that teens deep in "trig" *and* tots with their crayons can "fresh up" as often as they like!

Buy 7-Up wherever you see those bright 7-Up signs.

19

1953

The Middle East

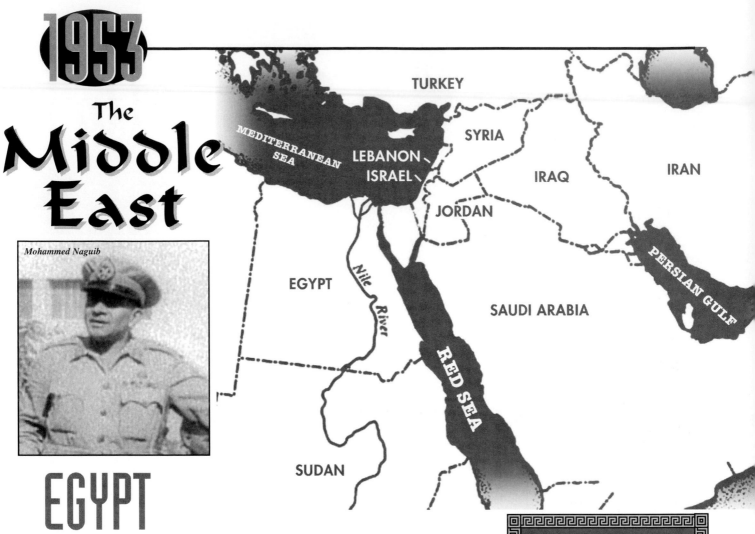

Mohammed Naguib

TURKEY

MEDITERRANEAN SEA

SYRIA

LEBANON

ISRAEL

JORDAN

IRAQ

IRAN

EGYPT

Nile River

SAUDI ARABIA

PERSIAN GULF

RED SEA

SUDAN

EGYPT

- Egypt's Revolutionary Council Abolishes The Monarchy And Proclaims A Republic Naming **General Mohammed Naguib** President And Premier.

- U.S. Joins Negotiations Between Great Britain And Egypt On Withdrawal Of British Troops From Suez Canal Zone.

- Following Disagreement On Basic Issues, Anglo-Egyptian Talks Regarding The Suez Canal Zone Are Suspended.

- Four British Destroyers And Royal Marine Units Are Sent To Suez Canal.

- 13 Former Aides To **King Farouk** Arrested In Cairo.

> ### U.S. Given "Choice" By Arab League Between Friendship Or Loss Of Strategic Bases In Middle East.

Two 18-Year-Olds Become Monarchs In The Middle East — KING HUSSEIN I Assumes The Throne In Jordan While His Cousin Becomes KING FAISAL II of Iraq.

Ex-Convict Assassinates PRINCE AZZEDINE BEY, Heir To Tunisian Crown.

WHAT A YEAR IT WAS!

IRAN

The Shah of Iran

- Asserting That His Life Is In Danger By The Power of Iran's **Shah Mohammed Reza Pahlavi, Premier Mohammed Mossadegh** Demands The Shah's Power Be Diminished.

- The Shah Flees Iran After Failing To Oust Premier Mossadegh.

- In Tehran, Mobs Riot As Supporters Of The Shah Of Iran Force Iranian Premier Mossadegh Out Of His Home.

- Americans Stoned In Iran By Mobs Shouting *"Yankees Go Home."*

- Shah Of Iran Returns Home From Baghdad After Government Of Mohammed Mossadegh Is Toppled By Troops Loyal To The Shah.

- President Eisenhower Announces $45 Million In Aid To Iran.

- Diplomatic Relations Resumed Between Britain And Iran.

- Iranian Ex-Premier Mossadegh Sentenced To Three Years In Prison.

Mohammed Mossadegh

ISRAEL

- U.S.S.R. Severs Diplomatic Relations With Israel After Bombing Of Soviet Legation.

- Labeling Zionists Agents Of U.S. And British Imperialists, Israel Is Considered Nonexistent In New Soviet Encyclopedia.

- U.S.S.R. Resumes Diplomatic Relations With Israel.

- The Mixed Armistice Commission And U.N. Condemn Israel After It Retaliates Against Jordan Following Jordanian Grenade Attack That Kills An Israeli Mother And Her Two Children.

- U.S. Joins In Condemnation Of Israel For Jordan Raid.

- **President Eisenhower** Sends **Eric Johnston** To Israel To Help Create Stability.

- Acceding To U.N. Request, Israel Ceases Rerouting Of Jordan River—U.S. To Resume Economic Aid.

MOSHE SHARETT Replaces Israeli Prime Minister DAVID BEN-GURION, Who Retires Due To Mental Strain.

LATIN AMERICA

Bomb Explodes At Rally For Argentina's President Juan D. Perón, Killing Six.

Juan Perón

Perón Accuses Three U.S. News Agencies Of Conducting A Campaign Of Lies Against Argentina.

One-Year Trade Agreement Signed Between U.S.S.R. And Argentina.

234,000 Acres Of Land Expropriated From United Fruit By Guatemalan Government For Land Reform.

In Bloodless Coup, General Rojas Pinilla Seizes Power And Takes Presidency In Colombia.

Eventually To Become A Self-Governing Unit In The British Commonwealth, British West Indian Colonies Announce Agreement On Formation Of A British Caribbean Federation.

Fidel Castro

26-Year-Old Lawyer Fidel Castro Leads 200 Armed Cuban Activists In Attack Against Two Army Barracks Near Santiago De Cuba Where Over 55 People Are Killed In A Failed Coup Attempt.

WHAT A YEAR IT WAS!

Africa

32 Die In Nigeria As Muslim Nationalists Riot For Independence From Great Britain.

Kenya

South Africa

In An Effort To Crush Civil Disobedience Against Apartheid, South African Parliament Passes Public Safety Legislation Granting Government Increased Power To Repress Minorities.

Alan Paton's Liberals And Federal Union Party, Anti-Malanist Parties, Are Formed In South Africa.

Alan Paton

Police Arrest 2,500 Tribesmen In Nairobi.

Anti-Colonialist Jomo "Burning Spear" Kenyatta, Leader Of The Kenyan Kikuyu Tribe, Sentenced To Seven Years In Prison For Leading Mau Mau Rebellion.

Barbed Wire Police Camp In Nairobi Is Site Of Biggest Mau Mau Attack To Date.

Koroseal BY B.F. Goodrich

Baby pants 49c to $1 · Play ponds $9.95 to $19.95 · Shower curtains $2.95 to $9.50 · Garden hose 50 ft., $9.80 · Raincoats $3.95 to $8.95 · Garment bags $2.50 to $4.95

Koroseal products shown, made by Kaybee Corp., New York

If they don't have the label they're not real Koroseal

Koroseal brings your family easier, better living

EVERY one of the things made of Koroseal in the picture above makes mother's work easier. Most of them brighten her kitchen as well—the matching set of curtains, table cover, shelving, shelf edging and chair backs and cushions. The trim looking apron and baby's bib are made of Koroseal flexible material too.

With Koroseal flexible material, spilled milk and most other foods and stains wipe right up. Even soap, grease, crayon and most acids won't harm it. Koroseal won't mildew, crack or peel—further proof that Koroseal flexible material is stronger and lasts longer than cheap washable or waterproof materials.

Koroseal also makes baby pants, raincoats, garment bags and shower curtains. And a heavier kind of Koroseal

flexible material is used for furniture upholstery that's washable and practically scuffproof. You clean Koroseal upholstery with a damp cloth or soap and water—it's like having new furniture a dozen times a year.

Look for products made of Koroseal when you want things that stay new looking, longer. But be sure you see the Koroseal label! *The B. F. Goodrich Company, Koroseal Division, Marietta, Ohio.*

Trade Mark – Reg. U. S. Pat. Off.

Koroseal
FLEXIBLE MATERIALS BY
B.F.Goodrich

Mr. Halfinsured's Crisis...
A CALAMITY IN 3 SCENES

Mr. Halfinsured's home was attacked by bad boys, all his lovely porch furniture smashed;

As he chased them away, a robber stepped up—in a flash Mr. H. was de-cashed;

When the maid took a powder— the silverware, too, the Halfinsureds learned these sad facts:

They had some insurance— but oh, what a shame—it covered just half of the acts!

You can be sure—that you are protected from loss with a Central low-cost Householder's Protective Floater. Insures property belonging to you or any member of your household against many perils —at home, at work, visiting, on vacation, or traveling! Send for free folder now.

Central
MUTUAL PROPERTY INSURANCE
DIVIDENDS TO PROPERTY OWNERS SINCE 1876
©1953

Household Inventory

CENTRAL MUTUAL INSURANCE COMPANY • VAN WERT, OHIO

● *Please send FREE folder describing the low-cost Householder's Protective Floater.*

Name _____
Address _____
City _____ Zone_____ State_____

PEOPLE — 1953

Harry S. Truman of Independence, Missouri stops for gas at Frederick, Maryland en route to visit Washington, D.C.

Harry S. Truman Pumps Gas

Like many other American tourists he says *"Fill 'er up"* to the gas station attendant, with whom he has a pleasant chat about his trip to the nation's capital.

The former president checks the dipstick, which shows the oil level is just fine.

All set, Mrs. Truman gets back in the car, followed by the driver.

He's now just another tourist heading east to familiar scenes in Washington, D.C. and *"no politics,"* says Mr. Truman.

1953 QUEEN ELIZABETH II CORONATION

Historic Westminster Abbey in London is the scene of colorful pomp and ceremony as Princess Elizabeth is crowned Queen Elizabeth II by the Archbishop of Canterbury.

Representatives from around the world attend the 2 1/2-hour ceremony while the people of the Commonwealth and British colonies hold their own daylong ceremonies.

Despite heavy rains, millions of people line the route for a glimpse of Elizabeth in her 4-ton gilded coach. Throngs of people are held back as they try to get a glimpse of the new storybook queen.

The hopes and hearts of England go out to this young queen and her husband, Prince Philip.

Royal Goings-On

An article appearing in London's *DAILY EXPRESS* claims that **Queen Elizabeth II**, who is about to turn 27, is a second cousin, seven times removed, to **George Washington** and a fifth cousin, five times removed, to **General Robert E. Lee** with the common ancestor being **Colonel Augustine Warner**, who settled in Virginia in 1628.

Queen Elizabeth II *dubs* **Winston Churchill** Knight of the Garter, Great Britain's highest and oldest order of knighthood.

85-year-old **Queen Mary** is reported recovering after a 19-day battle with gastric upset.

IN CASE I DIE BEFORE I WAKE — MAKE HIM KING

Queen Elizabeth II asks the British Parliament to amend the Regency Act to allow her husband, the **Duke of Edinburgh**, to become regent instead of her sister, **Princess Margaret**, in the event the queen dies before their son, **Prince Charles**, is old enough to reign.

A GIFT FROM HIS WIFE, THE QUEEN

Following his first solo flight, **Queen Elizabeth II** promotes her husband, the **Duke of Edinburgh**, to Marshal of the R.A.F., Admiral of the Fleet, Field Marshal of the Army.

Princess Margaret *causes a flap* when she goes strolling unescorted and, horrors, hatless with her Sealyham terrier in London's St. James's Park.

R.A.F. Group Captain **Peter Townsend** is transferred from the royal household to the post of air attaché in Brussels after the American press reports that **Princess Margaret** is in love with the handsome officer.

OH NO, NOT THE HATS

On a trip to Southern Rhodesia with **Princess Margaret** and 50 pieces of luggage, **Queen Mother Elizabeth's** hatbox is missing and winds up 600 miles away in Johannesburg.

THAT'S A WHOLE LOT OF SUSHI
Japan's **Crown Prince Akihito** gets $305,555.56 in spending money for his coronation trip and six-month visit to Europe and America.

BUT CAN SHE TYPE?
The Danish Parliament agrees on the text for a constitutional amendment that, if passed by both Parliament and popular referendum, would allow the ascension of a woman to the throne, paving the way for 12-year-old **Princess Margrethe** to be heiress presumptive.

ON THE CUTTING EDGE
32-year-old ex-**Queen Alexandra of Yugoslavia** cuts her wrists after she and 30-year-old ex-**King Peter** fail to agree on reconciliation.

Setting sail on the S.S. *United States* for a summer holiday in Paris, the Duke and Duchess of Windsor chat with newsmen and the former king announces that he will not be attending the coronation of his niece but will be building a hideaway in Versailles.

Queen Elizabeth II
AND THE
Duke Of Edinburgh
AT THE
Panama Canal

The steamer *Gothic* bearing Queen Elizabeth II and her husband, Prince Philip, enters the Panama Canal locks.

Her Majesty walks across one of the locks to observe the construction.

28

As the ship goes through Mira Flores, the queen is in the control room and pushes the lever that operates the mighty lock.

The huge gates open as the *Gothic* slowly inches out for the 50-mile canal trip.

With spectators looking on, Her Majesty then reboards the ship for the balance of her journey after viewing one of America's greatest engineering feats.

Her Majesty's compliments to the men who will take her ship to the Fiji Islands, 16 days away across the broad reaches of the South Pacific half a world away.

1953

BUDD ABBOTT & LOU COSTELLO

Lou rises to the occasion and decides to get a better look. He thinks all of the gals ought to win a prize, but he's ruled out of order.

Brenda Meigh of London is the winner and as Miss Great Britain she'll compete in the forthcoming world contest.

Prizes are a rose bowl and a check for £1,000.

First a kiss on the cheek from Abbott followed by a kiss from Costello who is knocked off his feet from all the excitement.

WHAT A YEAR IT WAS!

1953 ADVERTISEMENT

EVERYBODY wants
Congress Playing Cards...
because they're finer to handle,
lovelier to look at, game after game.
It's a pleasure to give a gift
you enjoy so much yourself!
CONGRESS Playing Cards CEL-U-TONE FINISH
Only Congress Cards have the incomparable
CEL-U-TONE FINISH
only CONGRESS
Playing Cards have CEL-U-TONE finish!
THE UNITED STATES PLAYING CARD COMPANY, CINCINNATI 12, OHIO. (In Canada, The International Playing Card Co., Winsor, Ont.)

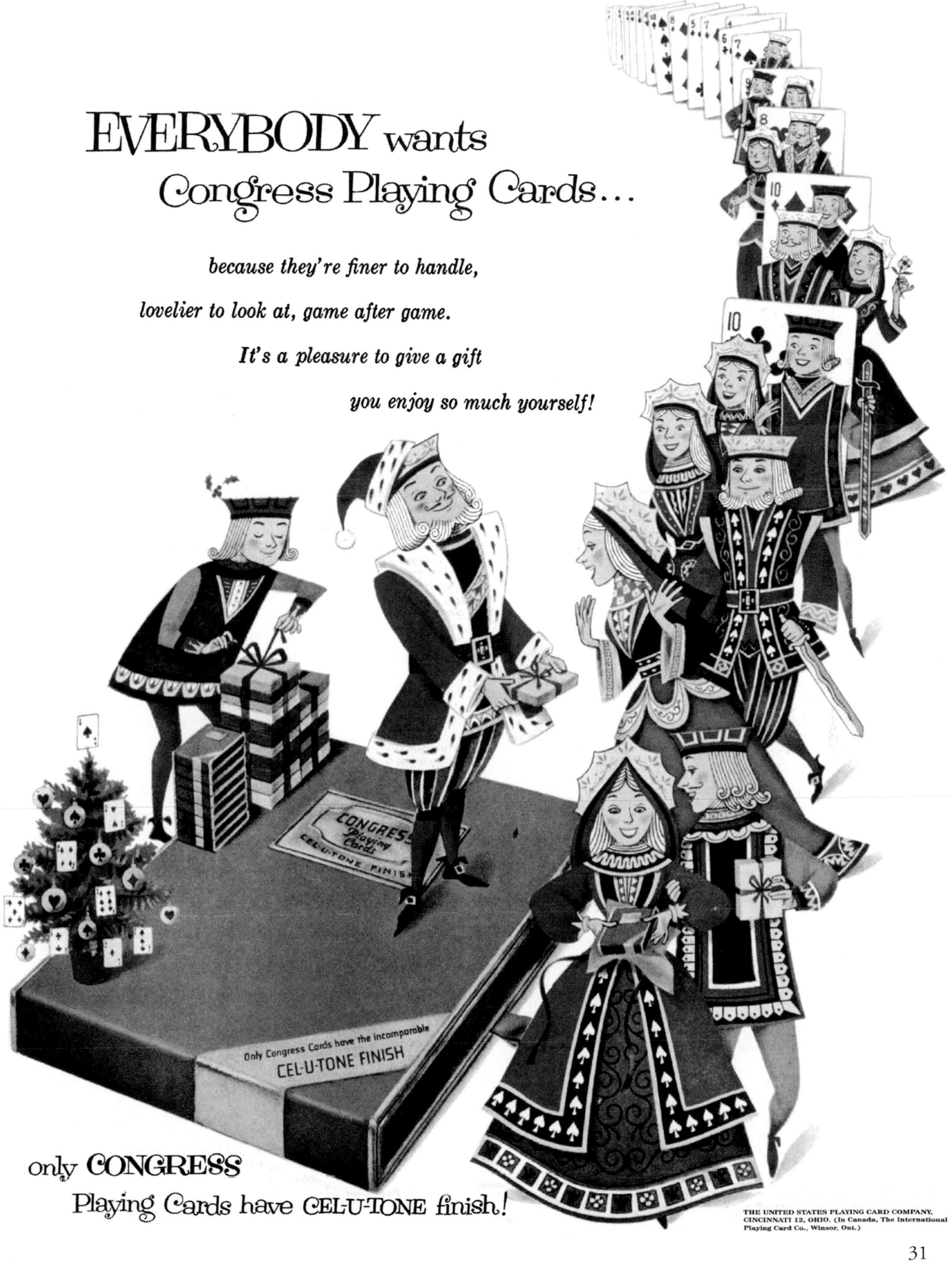

ENDING ON A LOW NOTE

Mario Lanza

*Tenor **MARIO LANZA** is being sued by his Hollywood landlady for $19,801 in back rent and damages.*

Frank Sinatra

LUCK BE A LADY TONIGHT

*With the IRS on his back for $109,997 in delinquent federal income taxes, **FRANK SINATRA** applies to the Nevada state tax commission for permission to buy a 2% interest ($50,000) in the gambling concession at Las Vegas' newest casino, the Sands Hotel.*

HE'S GOT THE I AIN'T GOT NO MO' MONEY BLUES

*Adding to his long list of woes, including debt, unpaid income taxes, deportation proceedings, alimony, etc., Argentine-born **DICK HAYMES** is expelled by Actors Equity, citing falsifying his birthplace.*

Marilyn Monroe, left, and Jane Russell

Ty Cobb

KEEPING HIS EYE ON THE BALL

Stating that he missed something in life by not continuing his education past high school, baseball's famous Georgia Peach, **Tyrus Raymond "Ty" Cobb**, sets up a college scholarship fund to aid three or four bright Georgia students.

THE SLUGGER SURVIVES THE SLUGS

On his first combat mission as a jet pilot, former Boston Red Sox slugger **Ted Williams** is struck by ground fire near Pyongyang but manages to get his jet back to the nearest air base where he survives a crash landing.

Declaring it doubtful that she would return to the convent, ex-film star **June Haver** returns to Hollywood after six months as a student nun at Sisters of Charity.

"America's Sweetheart," silent screen star **Mary Pickford**, turns 60 and is treated to a huge pink birthday cake at a birthday party thrown for her in Atlanta, one of the cities on her cross-country defense bond drive tour.

Girl Talk

In case you're wondering what Marilyn Monroe and Jane Russell discuss with each other between takes on the set of GENTLEMEN PREFER BLONDES, Marilyn discusses Freud and Jane tries to convert Marilyn to her religion. It is a philosophical standoff.

WHAT A YEAR IT WAS!

LINDBERGH

"The Spirit of St. Louis" is the title of **Charles A. Lindbergh's** memoirs and the SATURDAY EVENING POST is paying $100,000 for the rights.

IT'S A GOOD LIFE

LIFE magazine negotiates rights to former president **Harry S. Truman's** memoirs.

Harry S. Truman

83-year-old elder statesman **Bernard Baruch** attends ceremonies at City College of New York for the renaming of the School of Business the Bernard M. Baruch School of Business and Administration.

On a two-month Latin American lecture tour, 72-year-old **Helen Keller** is trapped by a storm for three days in a resort city in Chile but is rescued by plane under orders from **President Carlos Ibáñez del Campo**.

Tobacco heiress **Doris Duke** buys massive Hollywood hilltop villa, Falcon's Lair, one-time home of **Rudolph Valentino**.

COME ON, SNAKE EYES

Young, wealthy owner of 91 ships with offices in six countries, **Aristotle Socrates Onassis** acquires control of a famous casino and several hotels in Monte Carlo, Monaco.

Pulling up at Manhattan's Waldorf-Astoria in a gilded 1903 Ford wearing a 24-carat gold gown, Miss Tucker arrives to celebrate the **Sophie Tucker** Golden Jubilee Testimonial, honoring her long showbiz career, which began in her mother's restaurant.

Actress **Hedy Lamarr** becomes U.S. citizen.

The Stork Is Working Overtime

Lucille Ball and **Desi Arnaz** produce their second child, **Desiderio Alberto IV**, 8 lbs. 9 oz.

32-year-old musical comedy star **Carol Channing** has her first child—a hefty 9 lb. 2 oz. boy named **Channing**.

29-year-old Hollywood film star **Shelley Winters** and **Vittorio Gassman** have their first child— **Vittoria Gina**, 4 lbs. 10 oz.

Movie beauty, 20-year-old **Elizabeth Taylor** and her husband, **Michael Wilding**, have their first child—**Michael Howard**, 7 lbs. 3 oz.

Oona O'Neill Chaplin (28) and **Charlie Chaplin** (64) have their fifth child—a son—8 lbs.

Virginia Mayo (30) and **Michael O'Shea** (47) screen their first child— **Mary Catherine**— 7 lbs. 3 oz.

*Prince Aly Khan is ordered by a Reno court to pay actress **Rita Hayworth** $48,000 a year to support and educate their daughter, **Princess Yasmin**.*

HOW'S A GIRL TO MAKE ENDS MEET ON SUCH A PITTANCE?

Bobo Rockefeller, estranged wife of **Winthrop Rockefeller**, rejects $5,500,000 settlement.

K.O.'D IN THE FIFTH

42-year-old widow of financier **Harmon Spencer Auguste, Estelle** breaks off her five-day engagement to ex-boxing champ **Jack Dempsey** because he didn't approve of her friendship with **Kirk Douglas**.

Jacqueline Bouvier and **John F. Kennedy** announce their engagement.

1953

Coupling

Hank Aaron & Barbara Lucas

Mikhail Gorbachev & Raisa Maksimovna Titorenko

Hedy Lamarr & W. Howard Lee

Milton Berle & Ruth Cosgrove

Agnes Moorehead & Robert Gist

Henry Miller & Eve McClure

Pat Boone & Shirley Foley

Ann Blyth & James McNulty

Howard Hawks & Dee Hartford

Patricia Neal & Roald Dahl

Ann Rutherford & William Dozier

Jerry Lee Lewis & Jane Mitchum

Rita Hayworth & Dick Haymes

Clint Eastwood & Maggie Johnson

John F. Kennedy & Jacqueline Lee Bouvier

Roger Moore & Dorothy Squires

Cloris Leachman & George Englund

John Updike & Mary E. Pennington

Rosemary Clooney & José Ferrer

Ethel Merman & Robert Six

Lana Turner & Lex Barker

Sam Cooke & Delores Mohawk

Eunice Kennedy & Robert Sargent Shriver, Jr.

Louis Prima & Keely Smith

Sir Alexander Fleming & Dr. Amalia Koutsouri-Voureka

Ginger Rogers & Jacques Bergerac

Martin Luther King, Jr. & Coretta Scott

Sir Edmund Hillary & Louise Mary Rose

1953

Almost 3,000 spectators line up to catch a glimpse of society's top wedding of the year...

John F. Kennedy *Marries* Jacqueline Bouvier

The wedding of 36-year-old Harvard graduate and former PT boat commander, Senator John F. Kennedy, to 24-year-old Jacqueline Lee Bouvier is regarded as one of the year's most brilliant matches and recalls Newport's onetime social grandeur.

Former Ambassador and Mrs. Joseph Kennedy, parents of the groom, beam as they arrive at the church.

For the crowd outside the church it's a real storybook wedding. The radiant bride, formerly the inquiring photographer for the *WASHINGTON TIMES-HERALD*, is dressed in an ivory silk gown.

With a pretty wife and a politically rising star, the future is bright for the junior senator from Massachusetts.

WHAT A YEAR IT WAS!

Ills of the RICH & FAMOUS

FRANKLY, HE DOES GIVE A DAMN

Actor **Sir Laurence Olivier** brings his ailing wife, **Vivien Leigh**, back to England after she collapses in Hollywood from a nervous breakdown.

Passing

Queen Mary, 85 (Victoria Mary Augusta Louisa Olga Pauline Claudine Agnes)

TRIPPING THE LIFE FANTASTIC

Leading man **Alan Ladd** boards the QUEEN ELIZABETH in a wheelchair after breaking his ankle while playing with his six-year-old son.

+ Diagnosed with severe chronic osteomyelitis of the jawbone, **Bette Davis** has infected portion of the bone removed.

+ **Arthur Godfrey** takes sick leave from his radio and television shows to take care of an old hip injury.

+ Classical guitarist **Andrés Segovia** is recovering in a Madrid hospital following surgery for a detached retina.

ODE TO A SPOTTED FACE

On his spring lecture tour, **Ogden Nash** takes time out in Baltimore to recover from a case of chicken pox.

39-year-old golf pro and 1932 Olympics star, **"Babe" Didrikson Zaharias,** *undergoes surgery for removal of a malignant growth.*

NOW LISTEN, YOUR HONOR—
I NEVER LAID A GLOVE ON THE LITTLE LADY

Accusing each other of hitting the bottle and each other, Hollywood he-man **John Wayne** and his estranged wife, **Esperanza**, slug it out in a Los Angeles courtroom.

John Wayne

OH THAT THIS TOO, TOO SOLID FLESH...

Sir John Gielgud is fined $28 for *"persistently importuning male persons for immoral purposes."*

WAS HE OR WASN'T HE DRIVING UNDER THE INFLUENCE—ONLY THE BARTENDER KNOWS FOR SURE

A more than one-million-dollar lawsuit is filed against crooner **Bing Crosby** resulting from injuries sustained by three people in an accident involving Der Bingel's Mercedes-Benz.

Bing Crosby

THEY WALTZED OFF WITH ARTHUR'S DOUGH

The Park Avenue apartment of dancers ARTHUR & KATHRYN MURRAY is robbed and the thieves make off with $25,000 in jewelry and $150 in cash.

WHILE THEY WERE EATING

Burglars make off with over $19,000 worth of jewels from the bedroom of SIR LAURENCE OLIVIER and VIVIEN LEIGH as they are dining downstairs with their guests at their Buckinghamshire farm.

Frank Costello

MAMA MIA—I'M BACK

Racketeer **Joe Adonis** loses his appeal to the Board of Immigration Appeals and is deported back to Italy as an undesirable alien.

Getting time off for good behavior, gambler **Frank Costello** is released from federal prison in Milan, Michigan after serving 14 ½ months of his 18-month sentence for contempt of Congress but is immediately cited for speeding as he tries to get away from newsmen following his chauffeured Cadillac.

SEEING RED

1953

THE SENATOR DOESN'T GET HIS WINGS CLIPPED

The Senate Privileges and Elections Subcommittee charges **Joseph McCarthy** with being motivated by self-interest but does not remove him from his seat.

Under scrutiny for subversive tendencies yet denying any wrongdoing, **Charlie Chaplin** leaves the U.S. and heads to Europe where he surrenders his U.S. reentry permit.

THE HOLLYWOOD WITCH HUNT

In testimony given to the House Un-American Activities Committee, Hollywood actor **Lee J. Cobb** admits to being an ex-Communist.

Film and television star **Lucille Ball** admits registering to vote as a Communist in 1936 but testifies that she's never been a Red.

ENDING ON A SAD NOTE

Bandleader **Artie Shaw** becomes emotional as he testifies before the House Un-American Activities Committee that he had attended Communist meetings in 1946 and allowed his name to be used for Communist fronts.

Dancer-choreographer **Jerome Robbins** testifies that he was a Communist from 1944-47 and names other fellow members from the entertainment business.

President Eisenhower refuses to grant executive clemency to convicted atomic spies Ethel and Julius Rosenberg and they are executed.

Ethel and Julius Rosenberg

WHAT A YEAR IT WAS!

Of All The Girls In All The Countries...

In honor of making Swedish femininity beloved around the world, **Ingrid Bergman** receives a gold plaque in Stockholm.

The twin daughters of **Ingrid Bergman** and Italian director **Roberto Rossellini** celebrate their first birthday in Rome.

MISS AMERICA
Neva Jane Langley (Georgia)

BEST FAMILY MEN
IN THEIR FIELDS

Lt. General James H. Doolittle	*Humanitarian*
Alben W. Barkley	*Radio*
Rocky Marciano	*Sports*
Melvyn Douglas	*Stage*
Ezio Pinza	*Music*
Danny Thomas	*Cinema*
John Daly	*Television*

BROTHERHOOD WEEK

The **National Conference of Christians and Jews** honors the following people for promoting goodwill and understanding among Protestants, Catholics and Jews:

John Golden	Theatrical Producer
William Randolph Hearst, Jr.	Publisher
Walter D. Fuller	Publisher
Jack R. Howard	Publisher
Danny Kaye	Comedian
David Sarnoff	RCA Chairman

Danny Kaye

MOST ADMIRED WOMEN
IN THE WORLD
(Gallup Poll)

Eleanor Roosevelt
(4th consecutive year)

Queen Elizabeth II

Mamie Eisenhower

Clare Boothe Luce

Helen Keller

Mrs. Roosevelt

FATHER OF THE YEAR

Henry Cabot Lodge, Jr.
(U.S. Representative to the U.N.)

FATHERS' FAVORITE FEMALE

BEATRICE LILLIE

WOMAN OF THE YEAR
(Associated Press Poll)

Clare Boothe Luce

TIME MAN OF THE YEAR

Konrad Adenauer

WHAT A YEAR IT WAS!

Let's Play Conductor
$1.98
Other Let's Play Sets from 98¢

Finger Paint Set
$1.98
Others from 98¢

Hobby Craft Oil Painting
$2.49
Others from $1.19

Christmas Joy for Girls and Boys

America's TOP TEN TOYS!

Jr. Miss Cosmetic Case
$1.98
Others from 98¢

Plastic Teach-A-Toy Stencil Set
$1.98 Others from 98¢

Teach-A-Toy Plastic Map
$2.98

Dr. or Nurse Kit
$2.98
Others from 59¢

Mr. and Mrs. POTATO HEAD

the joyful toy of 1001 faces!

Jr. Miss Sewing Kit
$2.98
Others from 59¢

Hasbro Toys are truly inspirational — and there are none finer!
Designed for maximum educational play value,
a Hasbro Toy is a toy with a purpose.

Beaux Arts Paint Sets
$1.98
Other Paint Sets from 59¢

You'll find HASBRO *Toys*
Wherever toys are sold!

NEW
Mr. and Mrs. Potato Head
FUNNY FACE COMBINATION KIT

© 1953 HASSENFELD BROS., INC.
Pawtucket, Rhode Island

Mr. or Mrs. Potato Head
98¢ each

Mr. and Mrs. Potato Head
$1.98
Others to $2.98

Prices slightly higher west of the Mississippi and in Canada

Citing his honesty, experience and moderate philosophy, **President Eisenhower** appoints California Governor **Earl Warren** 14th chief justice of the U.S. Supreme Court.

In his first state visit outside the U.S., **President Eisenhower** visits Canada.

Ike names his brother **Milton S. Eisenhower** his personal representative on a goodwill and fact-finding mission to Latin America.

IKE

ALL THE PRESIDENT'S MEN *(and woman)*

John Foster Dulles

Secretary of State:
John Foster Dulles

Treasury:
George M. Humphrey

Attorney General:
Herbert Brownell, Jr.

Postmaster General:
Arthur E. Summerfield

Interior:
Douglas McKay

Agriculture:
Ezra T. Benson

Commerce:
Sinclair Weeks

Labor:
Martin P. Durkin

Health, Education & Welfare (new cabinet post):
Oveta Culp Hobby

Nathan Twining Takes Over As Chief Of Staff Of The U.S. Air Force When **Hoyt Vandenberg** Retires After 30 Years.

Ex-Air Force Lt. General **James H. Doolittle** Accepts Chairmanship Of The United Defense Fund, Which Supports The U.S.O.

Matthew Ridgway

Former Supreme Commander, Allied Forces In Europe, General **Matthew B. Ridgway** Named U.S. Army Chief Of Staff.

Allen W. Dulles To Be Promoted To Director Of The CIA.

Lt. General **Maxwell D. Taylor** Succeeds General **James A. Van Fleet** As Commander Of The 8th Army.

PRESIDENTIAL BACKUP

In his first speech since leaving the White House, former President **Harry S. Truman** encourages Americans to *"get behind the president and back him up so we can keep the peace of the world."*

HOW CAN YOU KEEP HIM DOWN ON THE FARM AFTER HE'S SEEN D.C.?

Addressing students at an Independence, Missouri high school, former President **Harry S. Truman** reveals plans to counsel high school and college students around the country on government and its functions.

OH THAT HARRY

Fumbling with his keys, former President **Harry S. Truman** accidentally sets off the burglar alarm at the Jackson County Courthouse where top-secret documents of his administration are stored.

In Her Easter Bonnet(s)

First Lady **Mamie Eisenhower** goes shopping for a new Easter bonnet but buys two instead of one.

Vijayalakshmi Pandit is elected president of the U.N. General Assembly, becoming the first Indian and the first woman to hold that office.

Following the ouster of Sultan Sidi Mohammed ben Youssef, Sidi Moulay Mohammed ben Arafa is proclaimed sultan of Morocco.

A MAN OF NOT TOO FEW WORDS

Senator **Wayne Morse** Filibusters For 22 Hours, 26 Minutes On Offshore Oil Bill—Longest Speech In Senate History.

71-year-old former Speaker of the House **Sam Rayburn** is honored at a Washington luncheon celebrating his record 40 years as a member of the House of Representatives, and historic 11 years as Speaker.

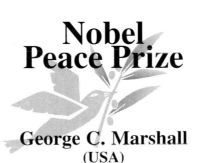

Vice President **Richard M. Nixon** Leaves On A Nine-Week Goodwill Tour Of The Far East.

Sam Rayburn

Nobel Peace Prize

George C. Marshall
(USA)

DAISY
The Waterskiing Dog

Meet Daisy and her trainer, Renie Renfro, standing on the dock at Lake Shasta, California.

Daisy, who has an odd name for a male, has the distinction of being the world's first waterskiing dog.

Yes sir, Daisy's quite a dog.
Look, Ma, no paws!

1953

LOVE & MARRIAGE GO TOGETHER LIKE A HORSE AND ???

Dr. David R. Mace, professor of human relations at Drew University in Madison, New Jersey, asserts that marriages based on romantic love alone do not last and that true marital success depends on physical, mental, emotional and spiritual harmony.

EMPTY CLOSETS ALL OVER AMERICA

PLENTY FOR WEDDINGS AND FRIED RICE
The U.S. rice crop sets a new record at 51,328,000 bags.

Young people are getting married in record numbers, according to Metropolitan Life Insurance, with marriages in the 15-24 age range hitting an all-time high.

AND SPEAKING OF WEDDINGS...

A total of 1,550,000 marriages are projected for this year.

A New York psychiatrist says that Americans have abandoned their idea that money is the key to a happy marriage and that the average person has four basic desires:
- To be understood
- To have emotional security
- To be loved
- To be recognized

JUST THE FACTS

POPULATION OF THE U.S. AS OF AUGUST 10th: 160,000,000

According to statistics released by the U.N., there are at least 900 cities worldwide with 100,000 or more people.

U.S. WIDOWS: 7,500,000
U.S. WIDOWERS: 2,500,000

Enrollment in 4-H clubs in the U.S. reaches an all-time high.

WHEW! IS IT WARMER IN HERE OR IS IT ME?
The average temperature for the U.S. in January is one degree higher than any preceding January for more than 50 years.

65% of U.S. households own a car with almost three-fourths of urban passenger travel being done by automobile.

YOU'RE NOT JUST SEEING RED
Color engineers at General Electric's general engineering laboratory estimate that the average person can see about 500,000 different colors.

Almost 400,000,000 flashbulbs are used by photographers this year.

frozen foods

20 lbs. consumed per capita

how sweet it is

According to the candy industry, 20% of candy bars sold cost 10¢.

U.S. per capita consumption of candy hits a low of 16.8 lbs. this year.

cholesterol heaven

Consumption per person this year:
Butter: 8.7 lbs.
Cheese: 7.7 lbs.

U.S. lifts price controls on wages and salaries and decontrols a large number of consumer goods including tires, gasoline, poultry and eggs.

Office of Price Stabilization lifts all remaining federal price controls on consumer goods.

holey wars

U.S. Agriculture Department sets standards permitting smaller holes in Swiss cheese.

Getting All Banged Up

The newest hairstyle in Washington is the "Mamie Cut" inspired by the First Lady.

✉ The U.S. Post Office begins experimental 3¢ airmail service between New York City and Chicago and between Washington, D.C. and Chicago.

☎ Researchers at Bell Telephone find that people making long-distance telephone calls tend to speak louder than on local calls, with the volume increasing 1 1/2 decibels for every 1,000 miles.

PINK SLIPS FOR THE DUMMIES

To be used as an "objective guide" in deciding whom to fire in an economy drive, 1,700 employees of the Foreign Operations Administration take an intelligence test.

spaghetti eating contest
It Could Take The Starch Out Of You!

New York is the site of the season's first and only Spaghetti Derby.

No hands, no silverware. Only schlurping allowed.

This saucy beauty is the winner!

Uh, oh!!
Things didn't quite pan out for this contestant, so she uses her noodle and crowns the winner herself, which takes some starch out of the two of them.

Thrilling!... PARK & TILFORD Perfume #3. Yet *surprise!* Costs less than many colognes! In jewel case, 49¢*

"Soaping" dulls hair...HALO glorifies it *with your very first shampoo!* 10¢, 29¢, 57¢, 89¢

Winter roughens your skin... PACQUINS Silk 'n Satin Lotion *satinizes* it! 25¢, 49¢*. In new dispenser bottle, 79¢*

SUSAN SMART† says

Hoping to go 'neath the Mistletoe?

Delightfully fragrant after bathing or when changing...a touch of CASHMERE BOUQUET Talcum. 12¢, 29¢, 43¢*

*Stays on!...*even when you kiss, eat, drink. It's HAZEL BISHOP Lipstick in Jumbo Swivel Case, 1.10*. Push-up Case, 59¢*

Your choice!... TONI Home Permanent in Very Gentle, Super, or Regular...according to your very own hair-type. Refill, 1.50*

Help that hope with a touch of holiday magic from

Woolworth's

array of toiletries

"Invisible shield" of FRESH Cream Deodorant helps keep underarms dry, odorless. 12¢, 27¢, 43¢, 63¢*

Gift idea! Christmas-packed GILLETTE Blue Blades in handy dispensers. Five 10-blade dispensers (50 blades), 2.45. 100 blades, 4.90

Never needs after-rinse!... LUSTRE-CREME Shampoo. And it's Hollywood's favorite for lovelier hair. 27¢, 53¢

It's the *new* TEK toothbrush...with the *new*, non-slip grip and the *new* tapered handle. 29¢

New shades for the new season! HELEN NEUSHAEFER Nail Polish in Joy, Gaiety, and First Lady Pink. 10¢*

Tests show LISTERINE Antizyme Toothpaste helps keep teeth immune to tooth decay acids *all day long,* in 9 out of 10 cases. 33¢, 59¢

*Plus tax
†Woolworth's Shopping Reporter

49

Little girls make big news in Long Beach, California. They're having a beauty parade. 100 of them between the ages of four and six are competing for the title Miss California Junior.

Miss California Junior Competition

Wearing the latest in small-fry fashions, these pint-sized beauties parade past judges and visitors to the annual California Society Picnic in Bixby Park.

Poise and personality are paramount and these little darlings have it all.

It's tough to choose, but 4-year-old Jane Rubble appears to be the winner and this little curly top is crowned California's Junior Miss.

CENTER OF ATTRACTION

PLAYBOY magazine hits the newsstands.

A weekly publication since 1888, **Collier's** announces it will now be published biweekly.

LOOK UP IN THE SKY, IT'S A BIRD... NO! IT'S A MOUSE

Selling 2,500,000 copies, the new 3-D Mighty Mouse comic book is one of more than a dozen 3-D comic books to hit the newsstands.

While 25% of the nation's newspapers refuse to print Alfred C. Kinsey's report, SEXUAL BEHAVIOR IN THE HUMAN FEMALE, the annual Newspaper Week is celebrated with the slogan "AN INFORMED PRESS MEANS AN INFORMED PEOPLE."

SPEEDING KILLS

A report presented to the Society of Automotive Engineers concludes that half of all traffic deaths are caused by speeding and that defective brakes cause more accidents than any other mechanical failure.

Chances are if you're driving your car at 65 mph you won't hear the siren of a motorcycle policeman until he closes in on your rear bumper.

While there are more female drivers today than in 1940, 70% of American drivers are still men.

CIVIL

Mexican women gain voting rights.

WIN SOME, LOSE SOME

The American Mothers Committee of the Golden Rule Foundation names a black stepmother, 58-year-old **Mrs. Ethlyn Wisegarver Bott**, of Belleville, Illinois, Mother of the Year.

For the second consecutive year there have been no lynchings in the U.S., reports the Tuskegee Institute.

GOING AGAINST THE BIAS

To discourage racial or religious discrimination, a 15-member Government Contract Committee is established by President Eisenhower.

HEY, WHERE DO I SIGN UP?

Florida's Grand Dragon of the Ku Klux Klan announces the organization will discard secret robes and rituals and open its ranks to "all races, creeds or colors" on a segregated basis.

In an effort to eliminate racial and religious restrictions on their membership, the State University of New York orders its fraternities and sororities to sever connections with national organizations.

The home near Diamond, Missouri of agricultural scientist **Dr. George Washington Carver** becomes a national monument, making him the first black to be so honored.

WHAT A YEAR IT WAS!

RIGHTS

Harvard Law School gives out the first bachelor of laws degree to women.

The Mississippi Legislature passes law providing "separate but equal" school facilities for black and white children.

Racial segregation of public high schools ends in Phoenix, Arizona.

Fisk University in Nashville is first black college to receive a Phi Beta Kappa chapter.

The Alabama Supreme Court rules that Creoles, early Louisiana settlers of pure French or Spanish descent, may not attend segregated white schools.

The U.S. Supreme Court hears oral re-arguments on the question of the constitutionality of racial segregation in public schools.

The U.S. Supreme Court rules that restaurants in the District of Columbia cannot refuse service to blacks "as long as they are well behaved."

The U.S. Supreme Court reverses a death sentence for rape imposed on a black man from Georgia, citing an all-white "rigged" jury. Justice Felix Frankfurter comments: "The mind of justice, not merely its eyes, would have to be blind to attribute such an occurrence to mere fortuity."

INDIAN AFFAIRS

Despite the objections of the American Civil Liberties Union, the Association on American Indian Affairs and the Navajo Indian Tribal Council, President Eisenhower signs a bill rescinding federal law and order authority over Indians, turning it over to individual states.

A federal law prohibiting the sale of liquor to Indians off reservations is repealed by President Eisenhower, allowing such purchases for the first time since the colonial days.

U.S. Congress declares for the first time that Indians should have all the constitutional rights of other citizens.

Navajo Indians of the Montezuma Creek area in Utah win a $100,000 federal court judgment for 150 horses and burros killed by federal rangeland officers.

1953

once upon a time in a little city called new york...

The $25,000 first prize in essay contest sponsored by General Motors on better highways goes to New York City Parks Commissioner.

New York City celebrates all year long the 300th anniversary of its incorporation as a municipality.

THE BETTER TO BAKE MORE COOKIES WITH

National Biscuit Company opens the world's largest bakery in Chicago, Illinois.

FRANKLY, THEY GIVE A DAM

In Texas, **President Eisenhower** and Mexico's **President Adolfo Ruiz Cortines** open the Rio Grande Falcon Dam with amity pledge.

Rockefeller family donates $6,000,000 for the construction of a guest lodge and cottages on Jackson Lake, Wyoming in the Grand Teton National Park to eventually house 5,000 tourists.

it's a-maz-ing

A mixture of smoke and haze—*smaze*—envelops the metropolitan New York area from November 17-22.

New York, as well as other major cities nationwide, is suffering from lost revenues as a result of the middle-class exodus to the suburbs.

BRIDGING THE GAPS

A $3,500,000 program is authorized for stiffening San Francisco's Golden Gate suspension bridge.

Construction begins on the $62,000,000 San Rafael-Richmond Bridge across the San Francisco Bay.

sailing, sailing

Italy's new ocean liner, *Andrea Dorea*, arrives in New York Harbor to much fanfare.

T-1, smallest U.S. Navy submarine built since 1910, is launched in Groton, Connecticut.

WHAT A YEAR IT WAS!

SEPARATING THE "ID" FROM IDEOLOGY

Acknowledging it another tool for modern healers, **POPE PIUS XII** approves psychoanalysis.

THE EARLY BIRD CATCHES THE YOU-KNOW-WHAT

An article appearing in THE SCIENTIFIC MONTHLY written by **Edwin Loeb** of the University of California says quoting proverbs excessively indicates a second-rate thinker and is also characteristic of the pathological or senile mind.

OLDER AND A LOT MORE WISER

Intelligent people appear to grow more intelligent as they age, according to a professor at the University of California.

A $3,500,000 program for advanced study in social relations and human behavior is announced by the Ford Foundation.

dem bones, dem bones

After 63 years, the remains of famed Sioux Indian chief **Sitting Bull** are moved from North to South Dakota to the site of the battle of the Little Big Horn.

Members of a British expedition, 34-year-old Edmund Hillary of New Zealand and his 42-year-old Sherpa guide, Tenzing Norgay, become the first to climb Mount Everest, the world's highest peak.

Cave Cougnac, containing prehistoric paintings, is discovered near Gourdon, France.

THE WEE FOLK
Danish **Dr. Tage Ellinger** reports the discovery of a pygmy tribe in Central Luzon, the Philippines.

A four-wheeled chariot and Greek and Etruscan metal vases are found in a tomb thought to belong to a wealthy Celtic person at Vix, on the Côte d'Or in France.

1953 *Legislation*

✑ The President's Commission on Immigration and Naturalization recommends a complete revision of the Immigration and Nationality Act of 1952.

✑ Teddy Roosevelt's Sagamore Hill home in Oyster Bay, Long Island is declared a national shrine as President Eisenhower designates the week of June 14-20 "Theodore Roosevelt Week."

Still Debating After All These Years

The Connecticut State Senate holds its 20th annual debate on a law forbidding the use of contraceptives by single or married women.

No Time Out For Daddy

President Eisenhower discontinues draft deferments based exclusively on fatherhood.

Extending The Quotas

President Eisenhower signs the Refugee Relief Act of 1953 allowing 214,000 additional refugees admission to the U.S. over the next three years.

Slick Subject

President Eisenhower signs the offshore oil bill granting coastal states rights to all minerals in submerged lands within their historic boundaries.

ONE HECK OF A HAY RIDE

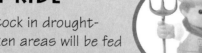

Livestock in drought-stricken areas will be fed this winter thanks to an additional $10,000,000 allotted by President Eisenhower for the transportation of hay.

KISSES NO LONGER NEEDED

Camp David, formerly known as **Shangri-la**, is the new name of the presidential retreat in Maryland, honoring President Eisenhower's father and grandson.

Harry S. Truman urges Congress to authorize special living expense tax deductions for the president, vice president and Speaker of the House.

Returning from a month's vacation in Hawaii with his wife and daughter, ex-President **Harry S. Truman**, citing national defense, urges statehood for Hawaii and Alaska.

Senator **Russell B. Long** endorses statehood for Hawaii, clearing the way for congressional approval. He had withheld his vote, demanding that the measure provide for Alaska statehood as well.

MAY WE QUOTE YOU ON THAT, MR. PRESIDENT?

For the first time in history, the White House allows the press to print direct quotations from a press conference.

from Photos to Sandpaper

...it's surprising how many ways
wood cellulose helps make your life more enjoyable and useful

Some of the happiest memories of your life are kept vividly alive for you on wood cellulose—in the form of photographic paper. To give you the sharpest, clearest snapshots, Eastman Kodak selects a highly purified wood pulp and transforms it into the finest of sensitized photographic papers.

At the other extreme is sandpaper. Ever wonder what makes it so strong, so tough, how it can take such a beating? Once again, it's that amazingly versatile material called wood cellulose—this time showing its more rugged side as sandpaper. Minnesota Mining & Manufacturing Company, one of the largest manufacturers of this paper of a thousand uses, looks to Brown Company, too, for cellulose fibres.

There's almost no limit to the applications of wood cellulose. Brown Company's technicians and service staff are available for consultation ... write Dept. GA-9 at our Boston office about your problem.

CELLULOSE is the basic material of all plant life. Its fibres form the tiny wood cells of trees. These fibres have amazing capacity to combine with other materials.

To produce cellulose from trees, machines first cut logs into small chips. These are "cooked" in huge pressure tanks with chemicals. Impurities are removed, and pure wood fibre results.

From this pulp Brown Company makes Nibroc towels and toilet tissue, Bermico pipe and conduit, Onco innersoles for shoes, and powdered wood cellulose called Solka-Floc. Brown Company also supplies highly-purified wood cellulose and specialty papers to other manufacturers to help make hundreds of familiar things you use every day.

BROWN **COMPANY, Berlin, New Hampshire**
CORPORATION, La Tuque, Quebec

General Sales Offices: 150 Causeway Street, Boston 14, Mass.—Dominion Square Building, Montreal, Quebec

SOLKA AND CELLATE PULPS • SOLKA-FLOC • NIBROC PAPERS • NIBROC TOWELS • NIBROC KOWTOWLS
NIBROC TOILET TISSUE • BERMICO SEWER PIPE, CONDUIT AND CORES • ONCO INSOLES • CHEMICALS

REMEMBER — ONLY YOU
CAN PREVENT FOREST FIRES

1953

Poster warns against "Red Menace."

which witch is which?

THE WITCHES HIT THE BOOKS

Reacting to head witch hunter **Senator Joseph McCarthy**, the State Department purges all its overseas books and materials by Communists. **President Eisenhower** warns against joining the book burners in a speech delivered at Dartmouth College wherein he says that you can't **"conceal faults by concealing evidence that they ever existed."**

Delivery of the October issue of **New World Review**, formerly **Soviet Russia Today**, is held up for three weeks by the U.S. Post Office pending its investigation into whether it contains disloyal material.

35,000 New York teachers receive a booklet entitled: **"Permit Communist Conspirators To Be Teachers?"**

In New York, 13 Communists are convicted by a federal grand jury on charges of conspiring to teach and advocate the forcible overthrow of the U.S. government.

Addressing the Friends Committee on National Legislation in Philadelphia, **Supreme Court Justice William O. Douglas** denounces *"the witch hunt and the merchants of hate."* He further condemns the growing underground of secret informers, saying that *"men are adjudged on the whispered accusations of faceless people not known to the accused."*

Marchers protest anti-Red fervor.

58

In a new executive order, **President Eisenhower** replaces the controversial Truman loyalty-security program with a stricter system.

Following the lead of **former President Harry S. Truman** regarding stricter controls on government security information, **President Eisenhower** orders uniform standards of "confidential," "secret" and "top secret" to all national defense material.

Following his refusal to comply with a subpoena from the House Un-American Activities Committee, **former President Harry S. Truman** defends his handling of espionage charges against former assistant secretary of the Treasury **Harry Dexter White**.

The Subversive Activities Control Board orders the U.S. Communist Party to register with the Justice Department as an agency of the Soviets.

A new executive order permits the discharge of any federal employee who refuses to testify before congressional committees by invoking the Fifth Amendment to the Constitution.

WHAT PRICE "FREEDOM"

Security inquiries result in 1,456 federal employees losing their jobs.

WAY TO GO, BILLY!

Illinois Governor **William G. Stratton** vetoes a bill requiring state and local government employees to take an oath denying membership in the Communist Party.

General Mark W. Clark

COMMANDER OF U.N. FORCES IN KOREA, GENERAL MARK W. CLARK, DEMANDS THAT THE COMMUNISTS RETURN OR ACCOUNT FOR 3,421 UNREPATRIATED U.N. PRISONERS OF WAR.

THE REDS MUST BE SEEING RED

A NORTH KOREAN PILOT SURRENDERS HIS SOVIET-BUILT JET FIGHTER TO THE U.S. AIR FORCE AT KIMPO AIRFIELD IN SEOUL.

THE HIGHEST-RANKING AMERICAN OFFICER TO BE CAPTURED DURING THE KOREAN WAR, MAJOR GENERAL WILLIAM FRISBIE DEAN, IS RETURNED TO THE ALLIES IN PANMUNJOM.

STAMPING OUT HIS IMAGE

All postage stamps bearing the image of **ex-King Farouk** are to have a black line drawn across his face by order of the Egyptian government.

THE ANGELS MADE THEM DO IT

After 99 years, France closes down its infamous, brutal Devil's Island penal colony, which imprisoned some 70,000 men over the years.

Danish people approve a referendum allowing a woman to ascend the throne and change the status of Greenland from a colony to a province.

Honoring the queen's coronation, 14,260 deserters from British armed forces during World War II receive amnesty from **Prime Minister Sir Winston Churchill**.

The West German Parliament passes a bill authorizing payment of $952 million to people persecuted by the Nazis on German soil.

Israel's **David Ben-Gurion** delivers his "abdication" address in a radio broadcast to the citizens of Israel.

Arabian pirates who seized the Indian vessel NARAM PASSA are captured by the British frigate FLAMINGO on the Arabian Sea.

The Chinese Connection

Merchant seamen smuggling heroin into the U.S. from Red China are blamed for the increasing narcotics traffic on the West Coast, according to Federal Narcotics Commissioner Harry J. Anslinger.

Sell A Joint— Get Your Head Chopped Off

The Turkish government passes a law making it a capital crime for trafficking in narcotics.

Iran's Parliament approves liquor ban.

They Ain't Just Whistling Brie Cheese

$500,000 in smuggled heroin is seized aboard the French liner FLANDRE by U.S. narcotics agents.

Let 'Em Drink Borscht

Soviets demand that U.S. stops distribution of $15 million of free food to East Berlin.

U.S. Air Force charges Soviets with trying to shoot down U.S. weather reconnaissance plane east of Siberian peninsula.

The Soviets open Moscow University.

A Striking Agreement

The British House of Commons announces a trade deal with Russia to exchange British woolen cloth for $1,400,000 worth of Russian matches.

Nine Jewish doctors in Kremlin arrested on charges of plotting to kill top Soviet leaders.

Not admitting mistakes very often, Soviet leaders free 15 doctors, 9 of whom are Jewish, accused of plotting against Stalin.

Associated Press correspondent William N. Oatis is freed in Czechoslovakia after being jailed for two years as a spy.

WHAT A YEAR IT WAS!

MAYBE WE SHOULD JUST STAY IN BED TODAY

A report released by the Health and Accident Underwriters Conference on occupational hazards indicates that while working as a baseball umpire is becoming less dangerous, acting in movies is becoming more dangerous. Ski instructors are less liable to accidents than stable hands, and bartenders and beauty operators are in equal danger. The most dangerous occupations are dynamiting, motorcyle riding and polo playing.

EXPANDING THE "UNION"

Western Union establishes a reservation bureau to help travelers find and book hotel accommodations.

Providing short- and long-range forecasts for 26 states as agent for the National Weather Service, Western Union expands its forecasting service to serve the entire U.S.

Designed to broadcast information to the public over the radio without giving enemy planes a signal to fix on, the CONELRAD defense system is tested nationwide.

UNICEF becomes a permanent agency of the U.N. and changes its official name to the U.S. Children's Fund.

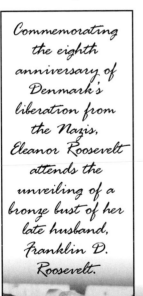

Commemorating the eighth anniversary of Denmark's liberation from the Nazis, Eleanor Roosevelt attends the unveiling of a bronze bust of her late husband, Franklin D. Roosevelt.

WHAT A YEAR IT WAS!

Oldest **Civil War** survivor, 111-year-old **James A. Hard,** dies in Rochester, N.Y.

1953

UNESCO
LITERACY REPORT
(Highest & Lowest)

Finland 99% (world's highest)
U.S.A. 97% (over 14 years of age)
Africa 1% (a sampling)

DOUBLE DECKER DESKS, ANYONE?

30 million American students will enter school in the fall—10 million more than schools can handle.

WELL, OK, BUT AT LEAST THEY CAN READ, CAN'T THEY?

National Education Association reports that a sampling of American school children scored lower in physical tests than a sampling of Italian and Austrian children.

- - - - - - - -

A NAME CHANGE

Yeshiva University Medical School changes its name to Albert Einstein Medical College.

GETTING THOSE SNAKES IN THE GRASS

With an unknown number of snakes slithering around Springfield, Missouri after escaping from an animal dealer or a traveling menagerie, 10 cobras are killed and the two-month search continues.

COULD IT HAVE BEEN THE RADIOACTIVE GRASS PERCHANCE??

More than 4,000 out of 11,000 sheep die while grazing near the Nevada nuclear test site.

61

Nothing, no nothing, is so important

Nothing you buy compares in importance with the things that protect your family's safety. Take tires, for instance. At today's speeds and in today's traffic, you need strong, blowout safe tires, able to stop quickly in an emergency. The General Tire is built to give you this extra protection.

THE GENERAL TIRE

DEBORAH KERR, currently co-starring in M-G-M's "JULIUS CAESAR".
In private life, this beautiful and talented M-G-M star is the wife of Anthony Bartley, Motion Picture Producer, shown here with their lovely daughter, Melanie.

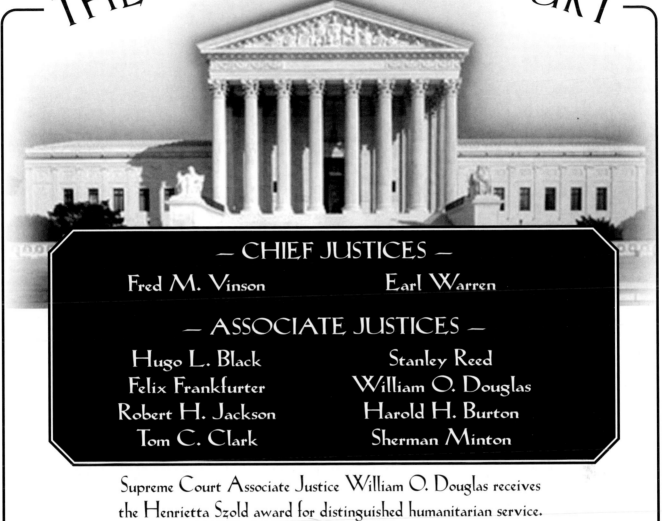

THE U.S. SUPREME COURT

– CHIEF JUSTICES –

Fred M. Vinson   Earl Warren

– ASSOCIATE JUSTICES –

Hugo L. Black   Stanley Reed
Felix Frankfurter   William O. Douglas
Robert H. Jackson   Harold H. Burton
Tom C. Clark   Sherman Minton

Supreme Court Associate Justice William O. Douglas receives
the Henrietta Szold award for distinguished humanitarian service.

Carl A. Hall and **Bonnie B. Heady** are arrested in St. Louis, Missouri on charges of kidnapping 6-year-old **Robert C. Greenlease, Jr.** for $600,000 ransom and his subsequent murder.

Testimony given before a joint N.Y. State legislative committee reveals that approximately $120 million of the more than $4 billion contributed to charity this year will end up in the pockets of racketeers and that 90% of charitable contributions to legitimate groups will end up in the pockets of professional fundraisers for fees and expenses.

DO YOU TAKE THIS WOMAN, AND THIS WOMAN, AND THIS WOMAN TO BE YOUR LAWFULLY WEDDED WIFE?

What is thought to be the last remaining location of widespread polygamy in America, almost the entire adult population of Short Creek, Arizona is arrested in a mass raid.

Israeli Premier David Ben-Gurion reports that 12.6% of the world's Jews live in Israel vs. 5.6% when the republic was founded.

The Jehovah's Witnesses baptize over 4,000 people at their world assembly held at Yankee Stadium.

records, records, we're breaking lots & lots of records

36-year-old French pilot Jacqueline Auriol becomes second woman to break the sound barrier when she dives her French Mystere II jet fighter at 687.5 mph over Bretigny.

A British Hawker Hunter fighter flies 727.6 mph, earning the Brits the world speed record.

In Los Angeles, Scott Crossfield flies at Mach II v—1,217 mph—in a Douglas D-588-II Skyrocket.

FASTER THAN A SPEEDING BULLET

Jacqueline Cochran becomes the first woman to fly faster than the speed of sound, simultaneously setting two world air records at California's Edwards Air Force Base.

Swiss professor AUGUST PICARD sets a record diving 10,330 feet in a bathyscaphe off the Italian coast.

A SOARING EXPERIENCE

U.S. Air Force and Royal Air Force pilots put on air show at Kitty Hawk, North Carolina commemorating the 50th anniversary of the Wright brothers' first flight in 1903.

According to British experts, jet plane flights will damage eardrums and wreck homes.

In a 6,170-mile hop from Kelly Base, Texas to Frankfort-on-the-Main, Germany, the world's largest plane, the six-engine XC-99, completes its first transatlantic flight.

WHERE'S A FINGER WHEN YOU NEED IT THE MOST?

A broken sea dyke floods a hangar on California's Terminal Island where Howard Hughes' giant experimental flying boat is housed, causing an estimated $5,000,000 in damage to the giant "airboat."

Sea Dart, the first jet fighter seaplane, is demonstrated by the U.S. Navy.

American Airlines *begins first regular nonstop transcontinental flight between Los Angeles and New York.*

WHAT A YEAR IT WAS!

New Words & Expressions

Subscriber Dialing
Someone who makes their own telephone calls.

Amble-Scramble
When pedestrians cross intersections in any direction.

Liner
Written material describing a specific artist or record, found on the back of an album cover or on the inner sleeve.

Superzoom Lens
A lens for a television camera that changes rapidly.

Telestudent
A student who learns from a broadcast.

Chain Reader
One who reads a lot.

Parabrake
A parachute used to help slow down an airplane.

3-D
Three dimensional.

Count-Down
Reciting numbers backwards before firing a missile or other such craft.

Phobiology
To gain information about phobias.

Triskaidekaphobe
A person who is frightened by the number 13.

Heavenly Hurricane
Fast winds at a high altitude.

Planicopter
An aircraft that is part airplane, part helicopter.

VTR
Video tape recorder.

Iron-Curtainland
Areas ruled by Communism.

Reactionary
What Communists call an anti-Communist POW.

Wumgush
Gibberish.

They give it First Place as the "buy" of the year!

New Clipper De Luxe 4-Door Sedan, one of 5 beautiful models in this great new line by Packard.

The New Packard CLIPPER

It takes a real BUY to stay hot all year! So don't miss a demonstration in the newest and most attractively priced car in the medium field!

An astonishing thing is happening on American highways today!

A new automobile is seen everywhere: its name is the new *Packard* CLIPPER.

Everywhere and in *ever-increasing* numbers. Literally, a success story in action!

The reason is *VALUE*—good, solid, substantial Packard value. Your money's worth.

So mark these words well: "Packard-built" really means something in an automobile.

It means that you get Packard engineering—traditionally fine, historically dependable.

Packard is the world's oldest and longest-respected name in quality motorcars.

It means that you get all the benefits in materials and workmanship that result from Packard's *quality approach* in motorcar manufacture—an approach that began with a very simple philosophy more than fifty years ago—*"How fine can we make it?"*—and continues on today.

From the famous Packard engine to the tiniest fitting on the dash, you can believe in Packard-built cars.

This is why the new CLIPPER, built by Packard, started in the news and has *stayed* in the news all year. More and more, you'll see them on the roads you drive.

Your Packard dealer will be glad to bring a new CLIPPER to your home or office for a demonstration drive. An hour or so in command of a CLIPPER will give you a new respect for quality in automobiles.

You will also see with appreciative eyes the full importance of the CLIPPER'S distinctive contour styling—one of the reasons *Packard-built cars are "the buy of the year" today* . . . one of the best reasons in the world why they will be the "trade-in value of the year" later on.

PRICES START AT **$2544.00***

*F. O. B. Detroit — Manufacturer's suggested price. State, local taxes and optional equipment if any, extra.

In addition to the Clipper, PACKARD is building today a car so beautiful and fine that it is applauded everywhere as "America's new choice in fine cars." Ask the man who owns one—today!

Arts&ENTERTAINMENT

MOVIES

a screaming success

Wearing special glasses, audiences have fun with the new 3-D films including **Bwana Devil** and **House of Wax** starring VINCENT PRICE, who is becoming the new international star of horror films.

NOTHING THAT HAS GONE BEFORE CAN COMPARE WITH THIS!

Beauty and Terror meet in your seat...as every thrill of its story comes off the screen right at you in NATURAL VISION

RIGHT AT YOU! The hand is at your throat...

RIGHT AT YOU! The kiss is on your lips...

RIGHT AT YOU! The horror that chills the spine!

3-DIMENSION

WARNER BROS. BRING YOU THE FIRST FEATURE PRODUCED BY A MAJOR STUDIO IN 3D!

"HOUSE OF WAX" WarnerColor

MUSIC

Benny Goodman returns to Carnegie Hall after 15 years.

TELEVISION

What's On Tonight, Honey?

With a picture of DESI ARNAZ, JR. on its cover, the first issue of **TV GUIDE** is launched and soon reaches a circulation of 1.5 million copies weekly.

TV GUIDE First Issue April 1953

Desi Alberto Arnaz IV

Ballroom Dancing

With songs such as **No Other Love** and **April in Portugal** on the pop charts, the popularity of the **tango** is stronger than ever, with the traditional **waltz** remaining the predominant favorite for dancers.

THE CRUEL SEA

THE DESERT RATS

DUCK AMUCK

FEAR & DESIRE

THE 5,000 FINGERS OF DR. T.

From Here To Eternity

GENTLEMEN PREFER BLONDES

Houdini

House Of Wax

How To Marry A Millionaire

INFERNO

Invaders From Mars

It Came From Outer Space

JULIUS CAESAR

Kiss Me Kate

Above And Beyond

THE ACTRESS

The Affairs Of Dobie Gillis

THE BAND WAGON

The Beggar's Opera

BRIGHT ROAD

Calamity Jane

CALL ME MADAM

THE CAPTAIN'S PARADISE

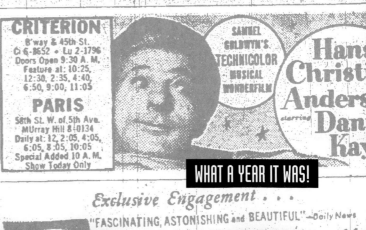

WHAT A YEAR IT WAS!

KNIGHTS OF THE ROUND TABLE
LILI
The Little Fugitive
Ma And Pa Kettle On Vacation
MARTIN LUTHER
The Maze
Miss Sadie Thompson
MOGAMBO
THE MOON IS BLUE
NIAGARA
Off Limits
PETER PAN
Pickup On South Street
Pony Express
THE ROBE

ROBOT MONSTER
Roman Holiday
SALOME
SHANE
So You Want A Television Set
Stalag 17
THE STOOGE
The Story Of Three Loves
TAKE THE HIGH GROUND
TARZAN AND THE SHE-DEVIL
THUNDER BAY
TITANIC
TORCH SONG
The War Of The Worlds
YOUNG BESS

1953

THUNDER BAY Premiere

The spotlight is on big-screen entertainment at New York's Times Square.

With a wide screen three times regular size, the gala premiere of *Thunder Bay* ushers in a new era in motion picture exhibition.

Directional sound heightens the entertainment value of the film, a saga about offshore oil drilling. The new wide screen, with its tremendous scope for panoramic thrills, lends itself to adventure films such as this.

Universal International executives are among the 3,000 people, including leaders of the motion picture industry, civic officials and stars of stage and screen, thronging into Loew's State for the world premiere of this history-making picture.

With New York's "Boys in Blue" controlling the crowd, fans line up to catch a glimpse of their favorite stars.

Maggie McNamara, who is covering this story, arrives with her husband.

Margaret Truman, *(top right)*, the **Boris Karloffs** *(center)* and **Xavier Cugat** and **Abby Lane** *(bottom)* are among the celebrities attending this historic opening.

Tony Curtis and **Janet Leigh**, Hollywood's popular "Mr. and Mrs." team, are greeted by their fans.

The star of the picture, **Jimmy Stewart**, arrives with Mrs. Stewart, his No. 1 fan.

1953

The Academy Awards

"And The Winner Is..."

Oscars® Presented in 1953

BEST PICTURE
THE GREATEST SHOW ON EARTH

BEST ACTOR
GARY COOPER, *High Noon*

BEST ACTRESS
SHIRLEY BOOTH,
Come Back, Little Sheba

BEST DIRECTOR
JOHN FORD, *The Quiet Man*

BEST SUPPORTING ACTOR
ANTHONY QUINN, *Viva Zapata!*

BEST SUPPORTING ACTRESS
GLORIA GRAHAME, *The Bad And The Beautiful*

BEST SONG
"HIGH NOON (DO NOT FORSAKE ME,
OH MY DARLIN')," *High Noon*

Gary Cooper

1953 Favorites (Oscars® Presented in 1954)

BEST PICTURE
FROM HERE TO ETERNITY

BEST ACTOR
WILLIAM HOLDEN, *Stalag 17*

BEST ACTRESS
AUDREY HEPBURN, *Roman Holiday*

BEST DIRECTOR
FRED ZINNEMANN,
From Here To Eternity

BEST SUPPORTING ACTOR
FRANK SINATRA, *From Here To Eternity*

BEST SUPPORTING ACTRESS
DONNA REED, *From Here To Eternity*

BEST SONG
"SECRET LOVE," *Calamity Jane*

Audrey Hepburn

WHAT A YEAR IT WAS!

FRANCE'S *Night of Stars*

President Vincent **Auriol** of France arrives to preside over the Sixth Annual Night of Stars.

Madame Le Claire, widow of the late general, is greeted by the French president.

A crowd of 5,000, including autograph hounds, jam the Tuileries grounds to catch a glimpse of **Charles Boyer** *(left)* and other motion picture stars to be honored for their work.

Among the stars to be honored is **Gary Cooper**, who for the moment abandons his he-man role and does a bit of mugging for the camera.

Gregory Peck gets the French equivalent of an Oscar® from the president as Americans play a prominent role in France's Night of Stars.

WHAT A YEAR IT WAS!

MORE FREEDOM DESIRED

After completing *Julius Caesar* and *The Wild One*, **Marlon Brando** announces that he is making one more film and that's it, citing his wish to travel and to develop a stage career where the censors have a lot less power over material.

FRIENDS, ROMANS AND ALL THAT SHAKESPEARE STUFF

Julius Caesar, starring **Marlon Brando**, **John Gielgud**, **James Mason** and **Deborah Kerr**, opens in New York.

Sean Connery finishes third in the tall man's division of the Mr. Universe contest.

The Beautiful Swan Doesn't Know She's A Beautiful Swan

AUDREY HEPBURN expresses surprise at being cast in movies, saying that she's had a complex her whole life about being ugly.

HARVARD'S LAMPOON AWARDS

Worst Comedian of All Time
Jerry Lewis

Worst Performance
Jerry Lewis
(JUMPING JACKS)

Worst Supporting Performance
Dean Martin
(JUMPING JACKS)

Worst Female Performance
Marilyn Monroe
(NIAGARA)

Marilyn Monroe

Martin & Lewis

WHAT A YEAR IT WAS!

TOP TEN
BOX OFFICE STARS

Gary Cooper
Dean Martin & Jerry Lewis
John Wayne
Alan Ladd
Bing Crosby
Marilyn Monroe
James Stewart
Bob Hope
Susan Hayward
Randolph Scott

Gary Cooper is voted this year's box office king.

Hollywood films enjoy great popularity with foreign audiences.

STARS
OF TOMORROW

Janet Leigh
Gloria Grahame
Tony Curtis
Terry Moore
Rosemary Clooney
Julie Adams
Robert Wagner
Scott Brady
Pier Angeli
Jack Palance

A new screen for drive-in movies, which gives three times the brightness of the screens currently being used, is developed by the Motion Picture Research Council.

NECKING TO A BIGGER SCREEN

Distribution of the new Todd-AO 3-D process is being handled by the newly formed Magna Theatre Corp., whose chairman and president are **Joseph M. Schenck** and **George P. Skouras**, respectively. Other participants in the new company include **Michael Todd** (process is named after him), **Richard Rodgers**, **Oscar Hammerstein II**, **Lee Shubert** and **Arthur Hornblow, Jr.**

Still retaining control of RKO Pictures, **Howard Hughes** sells his 929,020 shares of RKO Theater Corp. stock to a group headed by **David J. Greene** of New York.

The Robe is the first full-length dramatic motion picture to be produced in the U.S. using the CinemaScope process.

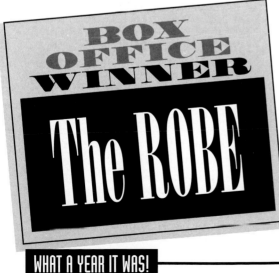

BOX OFFICE WINNER

The ROBE

Montgomery Clift is paid $150,000 for his role in *From Here To Eternity*.

HE FAILED TO PLEDGE HIS TROTH

MGM lawyers file a lawsuit against **MARIO LANZA** for $700,000 in production costs plus $4,500,000 in projected losses resulting from his failure to begin filming of **The Student Prince**.

NO MORE "BLUE" SKIES

Director **Otto Preminger** refuses to adhere to the MPAA movie code and distributes *The Moon Is Blue* himself. The film is a resounding financial success.

Painting With A Brush Of A Different Color

SALVADOR DALI announces his plans to produce a film next year called *The Wheelbarrow of Flesh*, starring **Anna Magnani**.

HERE COMES BIG BRO- THER

CBS airs Orwell's "1984" as a televi- sion movie.

FLYING HIGH

Walt Disney's  *premieres.*

COME ON, BOYS, IT'S ONLY A BREAST

Samuel Goldwyn urges the Motion Picture Association of America to allow *"a greater degree of latitude"* in its Production (decency) Code.

THERE'S MORE POPCORN IN YOUR FUTURE

The U.S. House of Representatives approves repeal of the 20% tax on movie admissions.

A TAXING ROLE

A loophole allowing highly paid movie stars and other rich people to avoid paying income taxes by living abroad 17 of 18 consecutive months is plugged up by the House of Representatives.

TIME TO PAY THE PIPER

Charging that they have been "blacklisted" from jobs in the industry, 23 film workers sue House Un-American Activities Committee and film studios to the tune of $51,750,000.

LINDY TRIES TO MAKE SAMMY HOP

Refusing to accede to **Charles Lindbergh's** demand for veto power over casting of the film based on his book, "The Spirit of St. Louis," producer **Sam Goldwyn** withdraws his $250,000 offer for film rights.

Charles Lindbergh

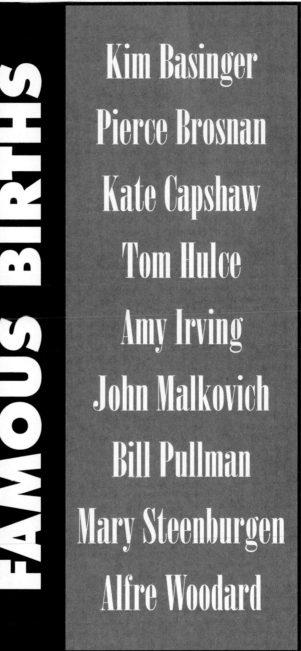

FAMOUS BIRTHS

Kim Basinger

Pierce Brosnan

Kate Capshaw

Tom Hulce

Amy Irving

John Malkovich

Bill Pullman

Mary Steenburgen

Alfre Woodard

Passing

Nigel Bruce (58)

Another Engineering Miracle by Emerson!

Presenting
EMERSON
21-INCH SCREEN
"SPACE SAVER"
MODEL 740
"PATENT APPLIED FOR"

"If I was Santa, I'd give us an Emerson for Christmas!"

NOW! A TV PICTURE SO CLEAR, SO DEEP
...you'll think you're at the movies!

FOR CHRISTMAS: SPACE-SAVER 21" MODELS!
Now! the *largest* picture in the most *compact* cabinet. Only Emerson has it...and you'll want your family to have it for Christmas!

READY NOW! AMAZING CINEVISION SCREEN.
As radical a television advance as 3-D is in the movies. Picture depth you've never seen before... plus the highest fidelity to sound yet achieved in TV! Whispers are clear...loud sounds *don't* boom.

SHARP AS A MOVIE, EVEN IN FRINGE AREAS!
Emerson's Dynapower Chassis *blocks out* interference. Emerson's Miracle Picture Lock holds the picture steady as a movie, too!

SIMPLIMATIC TUNING: ONE KNOB DOES THE JOB!
A twist of your wrist gets *any* channel. Every Emerson has a built-in antenna. Every Emerson is ready *now* for UHF. Choose from 44 distinctive models, priced as low as... **$149⁹⁵**

(Slightly higher in South and West)

THE SECRET!

Emerson's exclusive, revolutionary *side controls* make the Space-Saver Cabinet possible.

The front is all screen. A *full* 21" picture in the slimmest, trimmest cabinet ever built! *All wood*, in blonde, mahogany, and other fine finishes.

Emerson

EMERSON RADIO & PHONOGRAPH CORP., N.Y., U.S.A.

America's Best Buy!
Over 14,000,000 satisfied owners

What's Playing On TV

The Abbott And Costello Show	Jane Froman's U.S.A. Canteen
The Adventures Of Superman	The Life Of Riley
The Aldrich Family	The Lone Ranger
All-Star Revue	Mama
The Amos And Andy Show	Man Against Crime
Arthur Godfrey's Talent Scouts	Martin Kane, Private Eye
The Arthur Murray Party	Meet The Press
Beat The Clock	The Milton Berle Show
Beulah	Mr. Peepers
Big Town	My Friend Irma
Blind Date	My Little Margie
Break The Bank	Our Miss Brooks
Captain Video	The Perry Como Show
Cavalcade Of America	Pride Of The Family
The Dinah Shore Show	The Red Buttons Show
Dragnet	Rocky King, Detective
The Ed Sullivan Show	The Roy Rogers Show
The Ernie Kovacs Show	See It Now
Flash Gordon	Studio One
The Gene Autry Show	This Is Your Life
The George Burns And	Twenty Questions
Gracie Allen Show	The Walter Winchell Show
I Married Joan	What's My Line?
I've Got A Secret	What's The Story?
The Jack Benny Program	Your Hit Parade
The Jackie Gleason Show	Your Show Of Shows

Number Of U.S. Television Stations: 225 in 135 cities

LET COLOR BROADCASTING BEGIN

With the FCC due to approve specifications for commercial color televisions, Bizet's opera "Carmen" is televised on NBC-TV in color.

BLACK AND WHITE OR LIVING COLOR

RCA organizes the first coast-to-coast compatible color broadcast starring Nanette Fabray.

ALL SYSTEMS "GO"

The FCC rules color television can go on the air.

New Shows On The TV Block

Dr. I.Q.
Follow The Leader
The George Jessel Show
The Igor Cassini Show
The Larry Storch Show
The Life Of Riley
Life With Elizabeth
Life With Father
Letter To Loretta
Make Room For Daddy
The Man Behind The Badge
Marge And Jeff
My Favorite Husband
Name That Tune
Person To Person
Private Secretary
Romper Room
The Saturday Night Revue
Topper
The U.S. Steel Hour
Where's Raymond?
You Are There

Faces On The Boob Tube

Loretta Young

Robert Alda
Steve Allen
Don Ameche
Jim Backus
Ralph Bellamy
Charles Boyer
Joe E. Brown
Sid Caesar
Al Capp
Art Carney
Pat Carroll
Imogene Coca
Walter Cronkite
Melvyn Douglas
Mike Douglas
Ralph Edwards
Dale Evans
Alan Hale, Jr.
Conrad Janis
Audrey Meadows
Jayne Meadows
Edward R. Murrow
David Niven

Joe E. Brown

Jack Paar
Bert Parks
Ezio Pinza
John Raitt
Tony Randall
Ronald Reagan
George Reeves
Carl Reiner
Marion Ross
Ann Sothern
Dick Van Patten
Jack Warden
Natalie Wood
Fay Wray

George Reeves

Rod Steiger plays the forlorn butcher in the television version of **"Marty,"** which also stars **Nancy Marchand**.

Rod Steiger

NBC revives **"The Life Of Riley."**

"Riley" star William Bendix

HE DIDN'T GROVEL ENOUGH

Found "guilty" of overstepping his "boundaries," **Julius La Rosa** is fired by **Arthur Godfrey** on the air before millions of viewers.

TOP TEN TELEVISION SHOWS

Arthur Godfrey And Friends
Arthur Godfrey's Talent Scouts
Best Of Groucho
Dragnet
Gangbusters
I Love Lucy
Martin Kane, Private Eye
Racket Squad
You Bet Your Life
Your Show Of Shows

LET THE SNACKING GAMES BEGIN

56% of all American homes now have television sets.

Arthur Godfrey

WHAT A YEAR IT WAS!

MUGGING FOR THE CAMERA

Baby chimpanzee **J. Fred Muggs** gains national stardom thanks to his appearances on **Dave Garroway's "Today"** show.

Dave Garroway

81

1953

FAMOUS BIRTHS

TiM ALLEN

LOUiE ANDERSON

KEN BURNS

LAWRENCE HiLTON-JACOBS

PETER HORTON

DENNiS MiLLER

KEVIN NEALON

TONY SHALHOUB

Actors featured in television commercials will now get additional pay for repeated use of their images under new contract terms approved by members of the Screen Actors Guild.

75-year-old ex-Vice President **Alben W. Barkley** stars in "Meet The Veep," a new television commentary program emanating from NBC's Washington studios.

EXECUTIVE TURNTABLE

Sylvester L. (Pat) Weaver, Jr. takes over as president of NBC and **Robert Sarnoff**, son of RCA Chairman **David Sarnoff**, is new executive vice president.

American Telephone & Telegraph and Bell Telephone open a microwave radio relay channel across Lake Ontario, linking the U.S. and Canada for the first time.

NOT QUITE INSTANT REPLAY

Eight hours after the coronation ceremony of **Elizabeth II**, newsreels of the event, flown in from England, are aired on ABC-TV.

AND THE WINNER IS...

Live from the RKO Pantages Theater in Hollywood, the Academy Awards presentation is televised for the first time, over NBC-TV.

Lucille Ball

RICKEEEE, I'M READY

44,000,000, or 70% of the U.S. television audience, tune in to the birth of **LUCILLE BALL'S** baby on *I Love Lucy*.

The *I Love Lucy* show, No. 1 in viewer polls, is signed for $8,000,000, making it television's biggest single contract.

EMMY awards

SERIES

Situation Comedy
I Love Lucy

Dramatic Program
The U.S. Steel Hour

Variety Program
Omnibus

New Program (tie)
Make Room For Daddy
The U.S. Steel Hour

Mystery, Action or Adventure Program
Dragnet

PERFORMERS

Actor **Donald O'Connor**
The Colgate Comedy Hour

Actress **Eve Arden**
Our Miss Brooks

Supporting **Art Carney**
Actor *The Jackie Gleason Show*

Supporting **Vivian Vance**
Actress *I Love Lucy*

Outstanding Personality
Edward R. Murrow

WHAT A YEAR IT WAS!

1953 RADIO

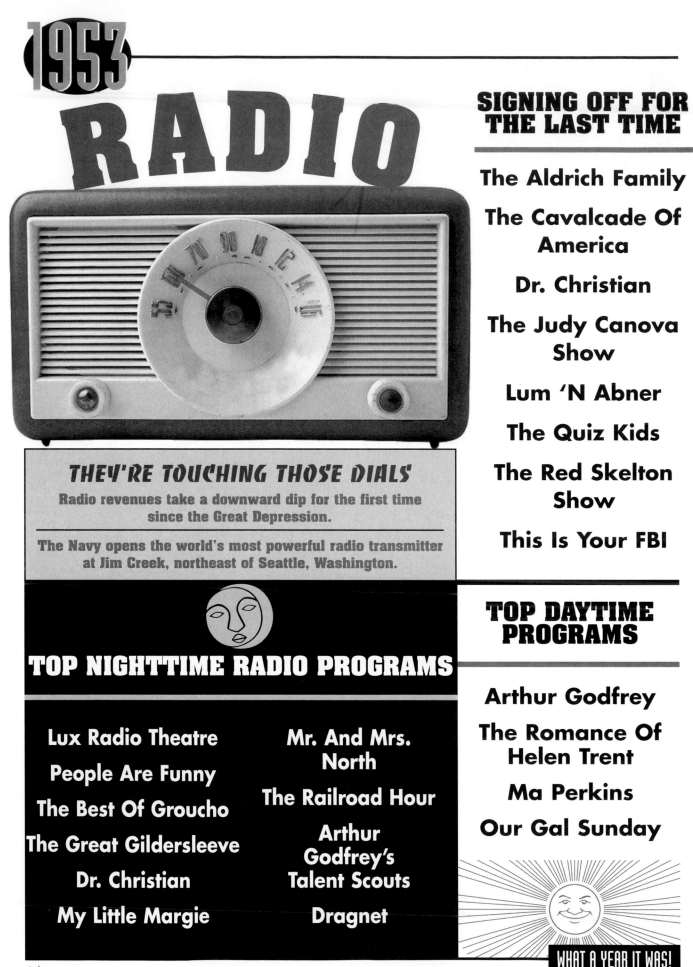

SIGNING OFF FOR THE LAST TIME

The Aldrich Family

The Cavalcade Of America

Dr. Christian

The Judy Canova Show

Lum 'N Abner

The Quiz Kids

The Red Skelton Show

This Is Your FBI

THEY'RE TOUCHING THOSE DIALS

Radio revenues take a downward dip for the first time since the Great Depression.

The Navy opens the world's most powerful radio transmitter at Jim Creek, northeast of Seattle, Washington.

TOP NIGHTTIME RADIO PROGRAMS

Lux Radio Theatre

People Are Funny

The Best Of Groucho

The Great Gildersleeve

Dr. Christian

My Little Margie

Mr. And Mrs. North

The Railroad Hour

Arthur Godfrey's Talent Scouts

Dragnet

TOP DAYTIME PROGRAMS

Arthur Godfrey

The Romance Of Helen Trent

Ma Perkins

Our Gal Sunday

WHAT A YEAR IT WAS!

A NEW VOICE IS HEARD

Advertising executive Leonard Erikson is appointed director of the Voice of America.

•

TUNING OUT THE VOICE

Suffering from congressional cuts, Voice of America programming has been either suspended or reduced.

•

SCRAWNY MOUSE CALLING BRIGHT EYED AND BUSHY TAILED

Thousands of radio amateurs participate in auxiliary civil defense communications work to implement the new Radio Amateur Civil Emergency Services to be used during national disasters.

TIRED OF SINGING "THE BLUE"

Deciding the public is bored with "*The Blue of the Night*," his radio theme song for the past 22 seasons, **BING CROSBY** orders the composition of a new piece of music.

WHO'S ON FIRST

61% of the estimated 27,500,000 homes with radios tune in to at least one of the World Series baseball broadcasts.

THE EARS OF THE WORLD ARE LISTENING

Broadcasting from 104 commentary points, 140 commentators describe the coronation of **QUEEN ELIZABETH II**, making it the most notable event in international broadcasting.

SLOAN SIMPSON O'DWYER signs a contract to host radio and television shows on WOR in New York.

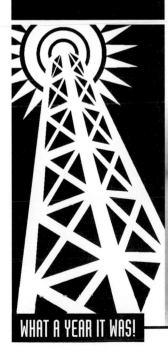

WHAT A YEAR IT WAS!

VELL, DAHLING, DO YOU ALWAYS VEAR THAT FUNNY HAT?

In what **The New York Times** calls *"the coup of the season,"* **EVA GABOR** receives a glowing review of her interview with **WALTER WINCHELL** on her late-night talk show.

Walter Winchell

Lamps selected by the Lamp and Shade Institute of America. Furnishings by the Grand Rapids Furniture Makers Guild.

The Before and After of G-E Light Conditioning

WHOSE lamp is it, "his" or "hers"? On the left, *before* General Electric Light Conditioning, it's hard to tell.

Look at the difference in the "after" picture on the right. Instead of two full-sized people bickering over one undersized lamp, G-E Light Conditioning has created a room that's labelled both "his" *and* "hers". Where reading, sewing, *every* seeing task is easier, more enjoyable. Where soft, even light brings out the beauty of draperies

and furnishings. It's actually a new way of living indoors.

Created by General Electric lighting engineers, Light Conditioning recipes tell exactly what kind of lamps to use for each seeing need. Show exactly where to put them. Specify the right kind of G-E lamp bulbs to use in them. Here's the "his-and-hers" recipe shown at right above:

"HERS": 1) *Swing-arm floor lamp with shade 16" across bottom, 47" above floor.* 2) *Placed so center of shade is*

15" *to left (or right) of sewing, 12" to rear.* 3) *Equipped with G-E 50-100-150-watt 3-lite bulb.*

"HIS": 1) *Table lamp with bottom of shade 15" above table, 16" across.* 2) *Placed 20" to right (or left) of reading material, 16" to rear.* 3) *Equipped with G-E 50-100-150-watt White lamp bulb.*

FREE! For your copy of a new G-E booklet, "See Your Home in a New Light", with 22 Light Conditioning recipes, write General Electric, Dept. 166-SEP-9, Nela Park, Cleveland 12, Ohio.

STUDY DESK RECIPE calls for table lamp placed 15" to left of work, 12" in from front desk edge. Equip with G-E 50-100-150-watt 3-lite bulb.

THIS FLOOR LAMP uses shade 18½ to 20" across, 49" above floor and a G-E 100-200-300-watt 3-lite White bulb. Often 32-watt circline fluorescent tube is added.

AVERAGE LIVING ROOM needs five lamps for pleasant seeing. Recipes No. 1, 2, 4, 5 (above) are from free G-E booklet "See Your Home in a New Light".

"Q" COAT in G-E White lamps gives softer shadows, less glare. Get choice of brightness with 50-100-150-watt (left) and 100-200-300-watt (right) 3-lite bulbs.

You can put your confidence in—

GENERAL ELECTRIC

POPULAR MUSIC

BIGGEST HIT OF THE YEAR

(*Lucky Strike Hit Parade*)

"I Believe"

Bill Haley's recording of "Crazy, Man, Crazy" is the first rock-and-roll song to make American national charts.

NEW RECORDING ARTISTS

The Drifters
The Flamingos
Marty Robbins

Singer Tony Williams forms new singing group named The Platters.

17-year-old Elvis Presley pays five dollars to record a two-sided single at Sun Records recording studio as a birthday present for his mother. A secretary, who is impressed with **"My Happiness,"** passes his name along to the owner of Sun Records, **Sam Phillips**.

Elvis Presley

graduates from L. C. Humes High School in Memphis.

Bill Haley & His Comets

WHAT A YEAR IT WAS!

POPULAR & HILLBILLY HITS

Anna
Silvana Mangano

April In Portugal
Les Baxter

Baby Baby Baby
Teresa Brewer

Baubles, Bangles And Beads
Peggy Lee

Caravan
Ralph Marterie

C'est Si Bon
Eartha Kitt

Changing Partners
Patti Page

Crazy, Man, Crazy
Bill Haley & His Comets

Dancin' With Someone
Teresa Brewer

Dennis The Menace
Rosemary Clooney

Doggie In The Window
Patti Page

Don't Let The Stars Get In Your Eyes
Perry Como

Don't Take Your Love From Me
The Three Suns

Dragnet
Ray Anthony

Ebb Tide
Frank Chacksfield

Eh, Cumpari
Julius La Rosa

Have You Heard?
Joni James

Hi-Lili-Hi-Lo
Leslie Caron

I Believe
Frankie Laine

I Confess
Perry Como

I Love Paris
Les Baxter & His Orchestra

If I Had A Penny
Rosemary Clooney

I'm Gonna Sit Right Down And Write Myself A Letter
Connee Boswell

I'm Walking Behind You
Eddie Fisher

In The Mood
Johnny Maddox

Into Each Life Some Rain Must Fall
Teresa Brewer

Istanbul (Not Constantinople)
The Four Lads

I've Got The World On A String
Frank Sinatra

Keep It Gay
Perry Como

Little Blue Riding Hood
Stan Freberg

Nat "King" Cole

Perry Como

WHAT A YEAR IT WAS!

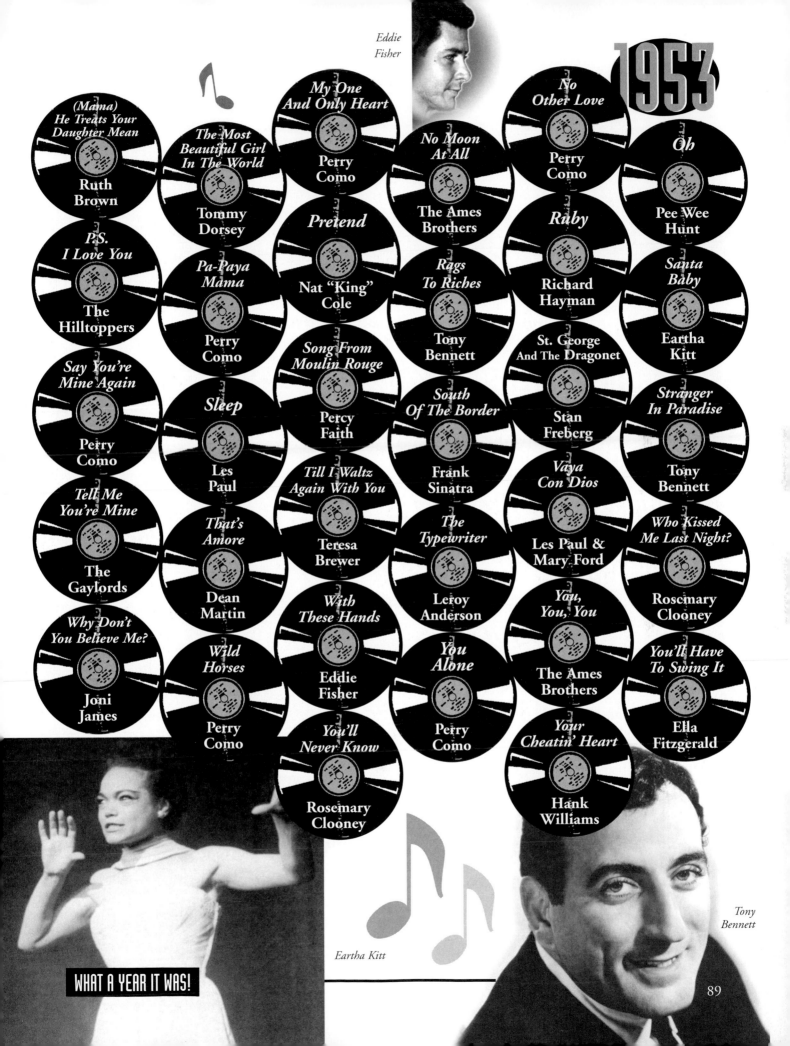

1953

(Mama) He Treats Your Daughter Mean
Ruth Brown

The Most Beautiful Girl In The World
Tommy Dorsey

My One And Only Heart
Perry Como

No Moon At All
The Ames Brothers

No Other Love
Perry Como

Oh
Pee Wee Hunt

P.S. I Love You
The Hilltoppers

Pa-Paya Mama
Perry Como

Pretend
Nat "King" Cole

Rags To Riches
Tony Bennett

Ruby
Richard Hayman

Santa Baby
Eartha Kitt

Say You're Mine Again
Perry Como

Sleep
Les Paul

Song From Moulin Rouge
Percy Faith

South Of The Border
Frank Sinatra

St. George And The Dragonet
Stan Freberg

Stranger In Paradise
Tony Bennett

Tell Me You're Mine
The Gaylords

That's Amore
Dean Martin

Till I Waltz Again With You
Teresa Brewer

The Typewriter
Leroy Anderson

Vaya Con Dios
Les Paul & Mary Ford

Who Kissed Me Last Night?
Rosemary Clooney

Why Don't You Believe Me?
Joni James

Wild Horses
Perry Como

With These Hands
Eddie Fisher

You Alone
Perry Como

You, You, You
The Ames Brothers

You'll Have To Swing It
Ella Fitzgerald

You'll Never Know
Rosemary Clooney

Your Cheatin' Heart
Hank Williams

Eddie Fisher

Eartha Kitt

Tony Bennett

WHAT A YEAR IT WAS!

89

1953

famous births

Pat Benatar

David Benoit

Danny Elfman

Chaka Khan

Cyndi Lauper

Shuggie Otis

Tom Petty

Alex Van Halen

passings

Django Reinhardt (43)

Hank
Williams
(29)

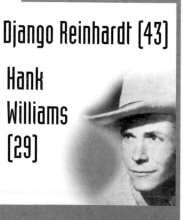

HIS BOOTS ARE MADE FOR WALKING

Crooner **Frank Sinatra** causes a near riot when he walks off the stage after singing one song at a theater in Naples, Italy and it takes the riot squad to calm the audience down and persuade Sinatra to finish his performance.

SPEAKING OF WALKING...

Frank Sinatra leaves Columbia Records and signs with Capitol Records.

Jimmy *(left)* and **Tommy Dorsey**, who split up in 1935, reunite and form a new orchestra.

Della Reese heads for New York to sing with the Erskine Hawkins Orchestra.

The *Staple Singers* cut their first recording.

Ella Fitzgerald is the first artist to sign with *Norman Granz's* new record label, *Verve.*

Atlantic Records brings in *Jerry Wexler* as its new vice president.

Dave Kapp, founder of Kapp Records, discovers **Roger Williams** playing in the lounge of the Madison Hotel in New York.

Roger Williams / Mr. Piano

WHAT A YEAR IT WAS!

merry music on a Webcor

There's no one in the family who wouldn't be just thrilled to get a Webcor fonograf this Christmas. When a person receives a Webcor for Christmas he has the added thrill of getting the fonograf that is wanted and known by those who really enjoy their music.

For instance, every Webcor fonograf plays all three speeds and all three-size records. The famed Webcor Balanced Tone Arm is a fonograf feature that means less wear on the delicate grooves of your records because only the exact minimum of needle pressure is applied. And, all Webcor fonografs and magnetic recorders come in sturdy, portable cases, finished to hand-crafted perfection in scuff-resistant, colorful luggage fabrics.

The Webcor Tape Recorder can help you capture Christmas morning for life—your first *precious memory*. Record your voice at your Webcor dealer's —it's fun and free, too.

Be sure to see your Webcor dealer this week; his selection is complete—from the tiny Midge at $29.95 to the glorious new, high-fidelity Musicale at $149.50.

All music sounds better on a
Webcor

Webcor is the brand name of the Webster-Chicago Corp.

Prices slightly higher west and subject to change without notice. © W/C 1953

MUSICALE...The new Webcor High-Fidelity Musicale gives you exclusive new Stereofonic Sound. THREE speakers, powerful amplifier and preamplifier and General Electric magnetic cartridge combine to provide 50 to 15,000 cycles of "live" performance sound. The finest sound from any phonograph today. In mahogany and blonde hand-rubbed cabinets. $149.50

HOLIDAY Completely automatic three-speed portable. Gives up to four hours of continuous music. Console response. Has a 3 tube amplifier, 5 inch speaker. $89.50

MAESTRO Beautiful 3-speed portable. Especially designed for the LP enthusiast. Bass reflex type cabinet. Lightweight. Handsome scuff resistant fabric. Rich tones. $59.50

TAPE RECORDER Over 40% of all tape recorders sold are Webcors. The reason . . . professional, high-fidelity recordings always. Two speeds, 3¾ & 7½. One knob control. $207.50

LARK Teenagers favorite. A handsome 3-speed portable with lifelike fidelity. Lightweight. One knob and tone control. Beautiful leatherette fabric. $39.95

MIDGE For your youngster. Extremely well built . . . with excellent tone quality. Plays 3-speeds. Easy to use. Weighs only 8¼ pounds. Three color combinations. $29.95

JUBILEE Beautiful table model. Plays all 3-speeds automatically in concert hall tones. 3 tube amplifier, 5 inch speaker. Decorator styled. In forest green or burgundy. $69.50

Classical Music

New Compositions

~

A Composer's World
Paul Hindemith

~

Concerto For Kettledrums And Orchestra
Gabriel Pierre Berlioz

~

New Frontiers
Heitor Villa-Lobos

~

Sixth Symphony
Peter Mennin

~

Seventh Symphony
(subtitled: "Sinfonia Antartica")
Ralph Vaughan Williams

~

Suite Hebraique
Ernest Bloch

VLADIMIR HOROWITZ *celebrates his silver jubilee with the New York Philharmonic.*

~

STOCKHOLM *presents its first music festival featuring a week of operatic and orchestral music.*

87-year-old JEAN SIBELIUS is named winner of the first international Wihuri Foundation music award and receives $21,250 in prize money.

Passing
———

Sergei Prokofiev
(61)

WHAT A YEAR IT WAS!

Opera News

Leonard Bernstein

New Operas

A Tale Of Two Cities
Arthur Benjamin

Gloriana
Benjamin Britten
(composed in honor of the coronation of Queen Elizabeth II, who attends opening night at the Royal Opera House, Covent Garden)

Joan Of Arc At The Stake
Arthur Honegger
(starring Ingrid Bergman in a non-singing role)

Les Mamelles De Tirésias
Francis Poulenc

The Marriage
Bohuslav Martinu

The Mighty Casey
William Schuman

The Rake's Progress
Igor Stravinsky

The Taming Of The Shrew
Vittorio Giannini

The Trial
Gottfried Von Einem

What Men Live By
Bohuslav Martinu

Volpone
George Antheil

Benjamin Britten

Igor Stravinsky

Leonard **Bernstein** conducts **Maria Callas** in Cherubini's opera *"Medea"* at the Teatro alla Scala in Milan, the first American to conduct in that famous opera house.

Leontyne **Price** sings **Sauguet's** *"La Voyante"* at the Metropolitan Opera.

27-year-old coloratura **Mattiwilda Dobbs** is the first black to win a principal role at La Scala opera house.

Metropolitan Opera kicks off its 70th season with **Gounod's** *"Faust."*

TEMPERAMENT FIT FOR A DIVA

28-year-old tenor **David Poleri** is fired from the New York City Opera Company for walking off the stage during a performance of *"Carmen"* in Chicago.

HELL NO, SHE WON'T GO

Undisputed prima donna of Italian opera, 29-year-old Brooklyn-born **Maria Meneghini Callas**, cancels her contract with the Metropolitan Opera to make her U.S. debut in *"La Traviata"* on the grounds that the U.S. consulate in Venice refuses to give her husband, Giovanni, a visa to accompany her.

Maria Callas

WHAT A YEAR IT WAS!

Dance

Alvin Ailey joins the **Lester Horton** dance company and takes over as artistic director following Horton's death.

The National Ballet of Canada makes its American debut.

The newly formed **Agnes de Mille** Dance Theatre begins a U.S. tour.

Galina Ulanova dances Swan Lake at Moscow's Bolshoi Theatre.

The New York City Ballet dances in New York, Los Angeles and San Francisco with **George Balanchine** choreographing Scotch Symphony, Metamorphoses, Harlequinade, Concertino and Valse Fantaisie. **Jerome Robbins** choreographs Fanfare with music by **Benjamin Britten** and Afternoon of a Faun, with music by **Claude Debussy**.

George Balanchine stages **Igor Stravinsky's** opera The Rake's Progress for the Metropolitan.

George Balanchine produces Le Baiser de la Fée at La Scala in Milan, Italy.

NO SWAN SONG FOR MARGOT

Following a bout with diphtheria last year, which caused numbness in her arms and legs, Britain's prima ballerina MARGOT FONTEYN makes her first appearance before a capacity audience at London's Covent Garden, where she receives 14 curtain calls and 41 bouquets.

SHE COULD HAVE DANCED ALL NIGHT

The Sadler's Wells Ballet, headed by MARGOT FONTEYN, performs five ballets never seen in America at the Metropolitan Opera House including *Sylvia, Homage to the Queen, Daphnis and Chloe, The Shadow* and *Don Juan.*

A DANCE FIT FOR A QUEEN

With choreography by FREDERICK ASHTON, Sadler's Wells Ballet produces *Homage to the Queen* in honor of the coronation of QUEEN ELIZABETH II.

New York's American Dance Festival features MARTHA GRAHAM in *Letter to the World, Appalachian Spring* and *Night Journey* and JOSÉ LIMÓN dancing in *Night Spell, La Malinche, The Visitation, The Moor's Pavane* and the premiere of *Deep Rhythm.*

A CHILLING EXPERIENCE

In London, ROLAND PETIT'S Ballets de Paris produces *The Lady in the Ice*, story and sets by ORSON WELLES.

THEY DANCED THAT-A-WAY

With guest artist MARINA SVETLOVA dancing, BORIS ROMANOFF choreographs *The Ballerina* and *The Bandits* at the Rome Opera.

WHAT A YEAR IT WAS!

ON BROADWAY

SAMUEL BECKETT'S "WAITING FOR GODOT" debuts in Paris.

BETTY HUTTON opens in a vaudeville show at the Palace in New York.

SIR LAURENCE OLIVIER AND VIVIEN LEIGH begin rehearsals in London for their new play, "THE SLEEPING PRINCE."

Alfred Drake
in *Kismet*

BIG BROADWAY HITS

CAN~CAN

Hans Conried
Peter Cookson
Lilo
Gwen Verdon

KISMET

Alfred Drake
Joan Diener
Richard Kiley

PICNIC

Arthur O'Connell
Eileen Heckart
Ralph Meeker
Paul Newman
Janice Rule
Kim Stanley

Josephine Hull
in *The Solid Gold Cadillac*

WHAT A YEAR IT WAS!

1953

David Wayne and
John Forsythe in
*The Teahouse Of
The August Moon*

THE *SOLID GOLD* CADILLAC
Josephine Hull

TEA AND SYMPATHY
Leif Erickson
Deborah Kerr
John Kerr

THE TEAHOUSE OF THE AUGUST MOON
Paul Ford
John Forsythe
David Wayne

WHAT A YEAR IT WAS!

OTHER OPENINGS ~OTHER NIGHTS

A DATE WITH APRIL
By George Batson

✵

BERNADINE
By Mary Chase

✵

CAMINO REAL
By Tennessee Williams

✵

THE CHILDREN'S HOUR *(revival)*
By Lillian Hellman

✵

THE CRUCIBLE
By Arthur Miller

✵

THE FIFTH SEASON
By Sylvia Regan

✵

HORSES IN MIDSTREAM
By Andrew Rosenthal

✵

KIND SIR
By Norman Krasna

✵

ME & JULIET
By Richard Rodgers & Oscar Hammerstein II

E. G. Marshall, Arthur Kennedy and **Beatrice Straight** in *The Crucible*

STILL DANCING AROUND

Former heavyweight champ **JOE LOUIS** plays to sellout audiences at a Harlem theater where he is featured in a dance review.

Actors' Equity Council votes that any member proven to be a Communist will be expelled from the union.

THE CURTAIN FALLS FOR THE VERY LAST TIME

A farewell party is held for New York's oldest playhouse—the Empire Theater.

THERE'S MONEY IN THEM THERE BOOBS

CHRISTINE JORGENSEN (formerly George) kicks off her entertainment career in Los Angeles starring in a vaudeville show at the Orpheum Theater.

Christine Jorgensen

THE MILLIONAIRESS
(revival)
By George Bernard Shaw

✵

THE PINK ELEPHANT
By John G. Fuller

✵

PORGY & BESS
(revival)
By George Gershwin

✵

ROOM SERVICE
(revival)
By John Murray & Allen Boretz

✵

THE SEVEN YEAR ITCH
By George Axelrod

✵

SHERLOCK HOLMES
By Ouida Rathbone

✵

TAKE A GIANT STEP
By Louis Peterson

✵

THE TIME OF THE CUCKOO
By Arthur Laurents

✵

TIME OUT FOR GINGER
By Ronald Alexander

✵

THE TRIP TO BOUNTIFUL
By Horton Foote

WHAT A YEAR IT WAS!

THE FINAL CURTAIN CALL

A RED RAINBOW

AN EVENING WITH BEATRICE LILLIE

ANNA RUSSELL'S LITTLE SHOW

THE CHILDREN'S HOUR

HAZEL FLAGG

JOHN BROWN'S BODY

MID-SUMMER

ON BORROWED TIME

PAL JOEY

ROOM SERVICE

THE TIME OF THE CUCKOO

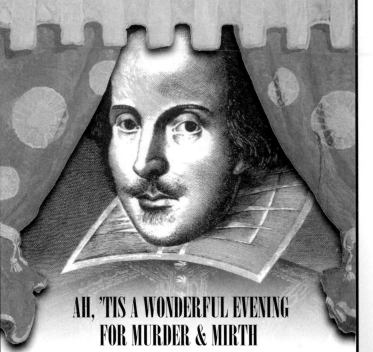

AH, 'TIS A WONDERFUL EVENING FOR MURDER & MIRTH

With over 53,000 people in attendance, the Stratford Shakespearean festival kicks off in Stratford, Ontario with **Alec Guinness** and **Irene Worth** starring in *Richard III* and *All's Well That Ends Well.*

AND FROM ACROSS THE *SEA* FROM LONDON

THE LOVE OF FOUR COLONELS
By Peter Ustinov

DIAL M FOR MURDER
By Frederick Knott

THE DEEP BLUE SEA
By Terence Rattigan

Rex Harrison in
The Love Of Four Colonels

WHAT A YEAR IT WAS!

TONY AWARDS
1953

PLAY
"The Crucible"
Arthur Miller (playwright)

MUSICAL
"Wonderful Town"

DRAMATIC ACTOR
Tom Ewell
"The Seven Year Itch"

DRAMATIC ACTRESS
Shirley Booth
"The Time Of The Cuckoo"

DIRECTOR
Joshua Logan
"Picnic"

MUSICAL ACTOR
Thomas Mitchell
"Hazel Flagg"

MUSICAL ACTRESS
Rosalind Russell
"Wonderful Town"

NEW YORK DRAMA CRITICS' CIRCLE AWARDS

BEST AMERICAN PLAY	PICNIC
BEST FOREIGN PLAY	THE LOVE OF FOUR COLONELS
BEST MUSICAL	WONDERFUL TOWN

SPECIAL AWARDS

BEATRICE LILLIE

DANNY KAYE

EQUITY COMMUNITY THEATRE

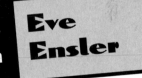

Famous Birth — Eve Ensler

Pulitzer Prize for Drama
PICNIC
William Inge

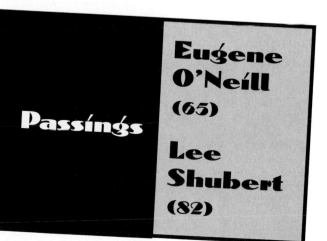

Passings — Eugene O'Neill (65) — Lee Shubert (82)

YOU PAINT WITH NUMBERED COLORS
A COLOR FOR EVERY NUMBER

SUBURB DE PARIS CM-29

"I painted it myself!"

YOU, TOO, CAN PAINT A BEAUTIFUL PICTURE IN OILS

THE FIRST TIME YOU TRY WITH AMERICA'S FAVORITE...

Craft Master

PAINT-BY-NUMBER OIL PAINTING SET

You don't have to be an artist . . . in fact you don't need any artistic ability at all . . . yet you can produce a beautiful professional-looking picture the first time you try. Start now, paint pictures for your home or for gifts. It's easy, it's fun, it's a grand hobby for everyone from eight to eighty.

here's all you do

Choose your favorite subject. You get 3 pre-planned, numbered, canvases and a set of pre-mixed, numbered, fine quality artist's oil paints

. . . then all you do is paint in the numbered areas with the corresponding numbered colors . . . easy isn't it ! You'll then have a beautiful oil painting that you will be proud to own.

3 Matching Pictures

are included with each Craft Master set and you can choose from 50 beautiful subjects for every home and every taste.

A Big Value!

Craft Master sets include everything you need to paint 3 beautiful pictures

complete for just **2⁵⁰**

You get a fine quality, 12 x 16 inch canvas and two matching 4¼ x 5½ inch canvases, a handy tray of permanent pre-mixed artist's oil paints (an average of 27 colors in each set), 2 artist's brushes and complete instructions.
Deluxe MASTERPIECE . . . with 18 x 24 canvas, 35 to 45 colors, 2 brushes and instructions 5.00

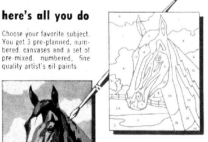

FREE!

Send for the beautiful 64-page catalog, in FULL COLOR, of the complete line. Shows how to hang pictures, etc. Include 10c in coin to cover cost of mailing.

NAME_____

ADDRESS_____

CITY_____ ZONE_____ STATE_____

Get your Craft Master and Masterpiece Sets **AT YOUR LOCAL STORE**

PALMER PAINT SALES CO.
Oak Park 37, Michigan

it's up to you
new york, new york

ART

Sculpture of the Twentieth Century is seen at the Philadelphia Museum, the Art Institute of Chicago and the Museum of Modern Art's new Philip Johnson-designed Abby Aldrich Rockefeller Sculpture Garden. Picasso's *Shepherd Holding A Lamb*, Calder's *Street Car*, Rodin's *John The Baptist*, Renoir's *Washerwoman* and Maillol's *The River* are included in the show.

Matisse bronze bas-relief

Matisse bronzes are on view at the Curt Valentin Gallery while his sculpture can be seen at London's Tate Gallery.

Robert Rauschenberg returns to the U.S. after studying in Italy and has a showing at the Stable Gallery.

An extensive Andrew Wyeth retrospective is held.

Due to striking guards, the Metropolitan Museum of Art is closed for 13 days.

Do You Dada?

A Dada exhibit is shown at the Sidney Janis Gallery.

Dada artists photographed in 1922. From top, l to r: Paul Chadourne, Tristan Tzara, Philippe Soupault, Serge Charchoune, Man Ray (inset), Paul Eluard, Jacques Rigaut, Mick Soupault, Georges Ribemont-Dessaignes.

WHAT A YEAR IT WAS!

1953

GUGGENHEIM NEWS

"Paris Through The Window" is shown, the first time a CHAGALL painting has been seen at the Guggenheim.

~

The museum purchases PICASSO'S "Mandolin And Guitar," painted in 1924.

Frank Lloyd Wright

With over 800 items, the FRANK LLOYD WRIGHT traveling retrospective is the biggest show of his career. The master architect designs the exhibition area to house models, drawings and additional items.

Edward G. Robinson's distinguished fine art collection is exhibited at the Museum of Modern Art and Washington, D.C.'s National Gallery of Art. Roualt's *Vase of Flowers*, Cezanne's *Black Clock*, Van Gogh's *Père Tanguy* and Matisse's *Les Desserts* join paintings by Renoir, Seurat, Corot, Toulouse-Lautrec, Morisot, Degas, Pissarro, Sisley and others.

Please, Johnnie's Finger Paintings Are Not Acceptable!

The British government now allows art to be used in lieu of cash to pay taxes up to $700,000 a year.

Okay, Students, This Is The Color Red

Cecil Beaton returns to art school to develop new skills.

Hey, Pablo, Can You Trim A Little Off The Sides?

The San Francisco Museum of Art will no longer accept paintings longer than five feet.

I Am Pablo The Great

The largest **Picasso** show in history is at Milan's Royal Palace and includes etchings, lithographs, ceramics, books, sculptures and paintings. Other Picasso exhibitions are seen in Rome, São Paulo, Lyons and New York.

A Smashing Success

The latest pieces of Steuben glass are designed by world-renowned artists including **Graham Sutherland, Henri Matisse, Salvador Dali** and **Jacob Epstein**.

Renoir's nude "Venus" causes such a furor in Portland, Oregon that the Portland Art Museum decides against buying the bronze.

Renoir's "La Fête de Pan" sells for $40,000.

With the help of a grant from the Rockefeller Brothers Fund, works by 12 modern American artists— including Jackson Pollock, Alexander Calder and Edward Hopper— are shown in Europe.

Alexander Calder

The Art Institute of Chicago mounts a comprehensive LÉGER exhibit, which then travels to New York and San Francisco.

An exhibit of MAN RAY paintings and collages, including "6,396,781," is on view at Paul Kantor Gallery in Los Angeles.

Perhaps the most unique group to sponsor an art event this year, Retail Drug Employees Union Local 1199 stages a one-man show of union member WOLF UBOGY, an amateur painter for many years.

GEORGIA O'KEEFFE paintings can be seen at the Colorado Springs Fine Arts Center's show, "Artists West Of The Mississippi."

New Works of Art

Georges Braque	*Apples*
Marc Chagall	*Eiffel Tower*
Alberto Giacometti	*Diego*
Joan Miro	*Painting*
Jackson Pollock	*Ocean Greyness*
Henry Moore	*Three Standing Figures*
Robert Rauschenberg	*Automobile Tire Print*

Andy Warhol **does illustrations for the book** *Madrigal's Magic Key To Spanish.*

Passings

Raoul Dufy (75)
James Earle Fraser (76)
John Marin (80)

WHAT A YEAR IT WAS!

The 100th anniversary of Vincent Van Gogh's birth is celebrated in the Netherlands with a major exhibition in the Hague.

105

Letters
can be
beautiful,
too!

IBM Electric Typewriters

INTERNATIONAL BUSINESS MACHINES, 590 Madison Avenue, New York 22, N. Y.
In Canada: Don Mills Road, Toronto 6, Ont.

Books

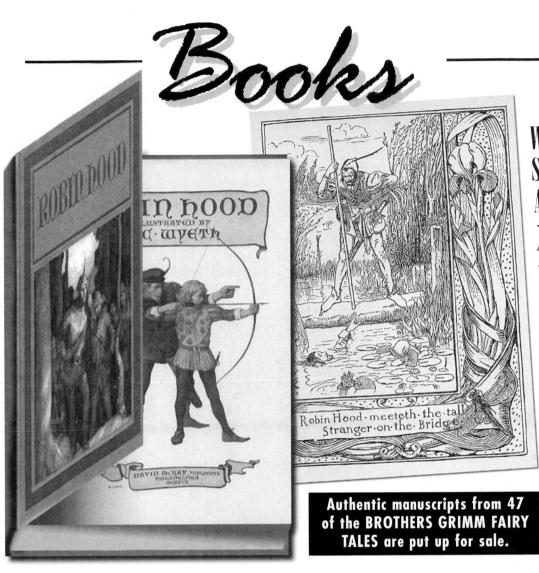

Authentic manuscripts from 47 of the BROTHERS GRIMM FAIRY TALES are put up for sale.

WHAT NEXT? IS SLEEPING BEAUTY A SUBVERSIVE?

A Republican woman on the Indiana Textbook Committee insists on having the tale of *Robin Hood* removed from books because Robin Hood's tendency to steal from the rich to give to the poor smacks of Communism.

National treasure **ROBERT FROST** is awarded a $5,000 fellowship by the Academy of American Poets.

T. S. ELIOT lectures on poetry for the National Book League.

WHAT A YEAR IT WAS!

The original copies of the **Constitution** and the **Declaration of Independence** are moved from the Library of Congress to the National Archives.

Poet Lawrence Ferlinghetti and Peter D. Martin open a little bookstore in San Francisco called City Lights.

CITY LIGHTS BOOKS

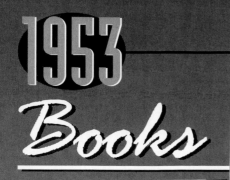

1953
Books

The Adventures Of Augie March
Saul Bellow

•

Always The Young Strangers
Carl Sandburg

•

Anecdotes Of Destiny
Isak Dinesen

•

An Italian Visit
Cecil Day-Lewis

•

Annapurna
Maurice Herzog

•

Battle Cry
Leon Uris

•

Beyond The Hundredth Meridian
Wallace Stegner

The Bridges At Toko-Ri
James A. Michener

•

Children Are Bored On Sunday
Jean Stafford

•

Come, My Beloved
Pearl S. Buck

•

The Dark Arena
Mario Puzo

•

Don't Call It Frisco
Herb Caen

•

The Dragon And The Unicorn
Kenneth Rexroth

•

The Enormous Radio And Other Stories
John Cheever

•

Fahrenheit 451
Ray Bradbury

Go Tell It On The Mountain
James Baldwin

•

The Hill Of Devi
E. M. Forster

•

i: six nonlectures
e. e. cummings

•

India And The Awakening East
Eleanor Roosevelt

•

Junkie
William Burroughs

William Burroughs

Life Among The Savages
Shirley Jackson

PASSING

Dylan Thomas (39)

Little Town On The Prairie
Laura Ingalls Wilder

•

The Lying Days
Nadine Gordimer

•

Nine Stories
J. D. Salinger

•

The Outsider
Richard Wright

•

Plexus
Henry Miller

•

The Private Dining Room
Ogden Nash

•

The Return Of Lanny Budd
Upton Sinclair

Science And Human Behavior
B. F. Skinner

•

Scrambled Eggs Super!
Theodor Seuss Geisel

•

The Second Foundation
Isaac Asimov

•

The Second Sex
Simone de Beauvoir

•

Seven Years In Tibet
Heinrich Harrer

•

Sexual Behavior In The Human Female
Alfred Kinsey

•

The Silent World
Jacques Cousteau

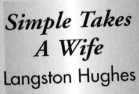

Jacques Cousteau

Simple Takes A Wife
Langston Hughes

•

The Spirit Of St. Louis
Charles Lindbergh

•

Such, Such Were The Joys
(posthumously)
George Orwell

•

Thurber Country
James Thurber

•

Triumph And Tragedy
Winston S. Churchill

•

Who Speaks For Man?
Norman Cousins

•

Zorba The Greek
Nikos Kazantzakis

NOBEL PRIZE FOR LITERATURE

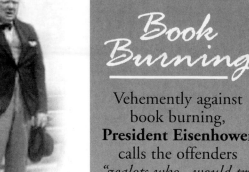

Sir Winston Leonard
Spencer Churchill

*"For his mastery of historical and
biographical description as well as for
brilliant oratory in defending exalted
human values."*

PULITZER PRIZES

Fiction	***The Old Man And The Sea*** Ernest Hemingway
History	***The Era Of Good Feelings*** George Dangerfield
Biography or Autobiography	***Edmund Pendleton, 1721-1803*** David J. Mays
Poetry	***Collected Poems, 1917-1952*** Archibald MacLeish

NATIONAL BOOK AWARD

Ralph Ellison   *Invisible Man*

POETRY SOCIETY OF AMERICA
GOLD MEDAL

Carl Sandburg

BOLLINGEN POETRY PRIZE

Archibald MacLeish

William Carlos Williams

Book Burning

Vehemently against book burning, **President Eisenhower** calls the offenders *"zealots who...would try to defend freedom by denying freedom's friends the opportunity of studying Communism."*

Addressing the same topic at Dartmouth College, the president urges, *"Don't join the book burners. Don't think you are going to conceal thoughts by concealing evidence that they ever existed.... How will we defeat Communism unless we know what it is and why it has such an appeal for men?... We have got to fight it with some-thing better, not try to conceal it."*

The National Education Association condemns *"book burn-ings, purges or other devices which restrict freedom of thought."*

WHAT A YEAR IT WAS!

Fashion—1953

Rome
FASHION SHOW

Four of Italy's leading designers pool their talents in a showing of evening attire in hopes of gaining the title of fashion capital of the world.

In Paris, New York, Rome, whichever city you insist is the world's fashion capital, no wardrobe is complete without a fur coat and neither is a fashion show. So, here is a beautiful finish to fashion finery.

1953 — NEW YORK'S TOP DESIGNERS

*N*ew York's top designers get together to create just one complete outfit to clothe just one girl who they've named the **"Million-Dollar Baby."**

*H*ere's our unadorned model.

*F*irst the feet. These are satin strapped sandals by I. Miller Shoes. Price Tag: $50.

"ca-ching"

*N*ext we adorn our Million-Dollar Baby with Van Cleef and Arpel's diamond necklace, earrings, bracelets, pin and ring. Price Tag: $500,000.

"ca-ching"
"ca-ching"

WHAT A YEAR IT WAS!

CREATE MILLION-DOLLAR BABY—1953

*S*ociety milliner Mr. John creates a black silk velvet cocktail chapeau with black egret feathers. Price Tag: $500.

"ca-ching"
"ca-ching"

*N*etty Rosenstein's contribution is this black velvet evening dress with a winged neckline, halter neck and full skirt. Beautifully simple, isn't it? Price Tag: $400.

"ca-ching"

*T*o wrap it up, a royal pastel mink designed by Miss Ruth Ruddy *(below)*. Price Tag: $25,000.
GRAND TOTAL: $525,950.
(O.K., so it's not quite a million.)

1953

FASHIONS ON PARADE TO AID THE

MARCH OF DIMES

This four-year-old young man, next year's polio poster boy, takes the spotlight as he is escorted on stage by these lovely young ladies to open the 10th Annual March of Dimes Fashion Show presented by the New York Press Institute for the benefit of the National Foundation for Infantile Paralysis.

Actress Helen Hayes (left) is seated with Basil O'Connor, president of the national foundation, which is supported by many celebrities.

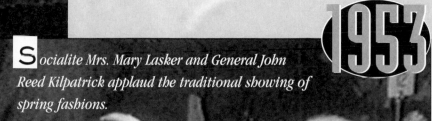

1953

Socialite Mrs. Mary Lasker and General John Reed Kilpatrick applaud the traditional showing of spring fashions.

Featured throughout the showing is the winged victory silhouette, so-called to symbolize the hope of winning the battle against polio.

It's a thrilling first glimpse of this spring's styles with the added virtue of serving a very good cause.

WHAT A YEAR IT WAS!

Their Idea... Nail enamel and lipstick colors, said Revlon, could become costume accessories. In 1932, with $300 capital, they mixed their first batch of nail enamel. In 1935, they grossed $68,000. "Idea men," left to right: Charles Revson, Charles Lachman, Martin and Joseph Revson.

Can Business Success Be Built On Emotion?

Revlon Products Corporation bets bottom dollar on women's moods...gross leaps from hundreds to millions with Journal carrying heavy schedule of advertising

The Revson brothers—Charles, Joseph and Martin—and their partner, Charles Lachman, staked their shirts on something many men would consider an incalculable risk—*women's emotions.*

Yet it paid off. A revolutionary idea—the introduction of a wide range of fresh new shades in nail enamel—plus determination and back-breaking work, have netted Revlon a business which would make the average steel magnate blink.

Since the first big-scale Revlon advertising in 1936, magazines have carried the main weight of it. *And the Journal holds top position on the Revlon list.*

Referring to the promotional strength of the greatest magazine ever edited for women, Mr. Charles Revson, President, says:

"The Journal gets into a greater spread of homes than any other women's magazine in the world, and gets real response."

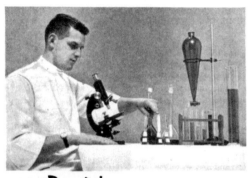

Was Dramatic! Until 1932, nail polish shades were few. Today Revlon has 31 shades of nail enamel with matching lipsticks, and unerringly hits the right fashion shade seven months ahead of the retail season. Revlon is the giant of *all* cosmetic firms that sell through retail outlets.

Their Approach... In 1937, Revlon entered the department store field. B. Altman & Co. was one of the few "trial" stores. Today, every leading store in the country carries the dramatic Revlon line. Pictured is the Spring, 1953, counter at B. Altman & Co., New York.

Was Different! Always advertised in high-fashion surroundings, Revlon quickly became a symbol of glamour and hope to all women. At right, Revlon's famous Fire-and-Ice girl. Revlon also makes hand lotion, face powder, rouge, all types of make-up and face cream, a whole beauty treatment line.

Women went for it! Inevitably, when an advertiser wants to reach the *most* women with the *most buying power,* he turns to Ladies' Home Journal—which gives him

1. *Top circulation* of any monthly magazine in the world carrying advertising . . .
2. *Top newsstand sales* of any magazine in the world carrying advertising.

Ladies' Home **Journal**

...the magazine women believe in

A Curtis Publication

The first **GUCCI** store outside of Italy is opened in New York City by founder **Guccio Gucci's** sons, **Rodolfo** and **Aldo**.

MISSONI is formed in Italy by newlyweds **Ottavio** and **Rosita Missoni**.

Wool continues to be one of the most preferred fabrics in the U.S. A new material, **polyester**, is introduced into the marketplace.

A pregnant woman named *Laura Ashley* begins silk-screening scarves in her kitchen.

Queen Elizabeth's white satin coronation gown, designed by London's Norman Hartnell, weighs in at 30 pounds, replete with diamonds, pearls, crystals and 10 petticoats.

In the first televised Academy Awards ceremony, EDITH HEAD *is the fashion adviser who helps celebrities pick their attire and makes sure they are dressed modestly enough for television.*

THE FASHION WORLD LOOKS TO PARIS—AGAIN

Lanvin-Castillo, **Givenchy, Fath** and **Schiaparelli** all make their own versions of the latest tweed suit.

Hubert Givenchy and **Audrey Hepburn** meet for the first time and become instant friends.

Givenchy boutiques open in Zurich, Buenos Aires and Rome.

17-year-old **Yves St. Laurent** has some of his sketches published in **Vogue.**

St. Laurent goes to work for **Christian Dior** as his assistant.

Christian Dior raises hemlines to 15 ¹/₂" from the floor.

Narrow evening dresses, sometimes with a bare shoulder or two.

Party Dresses

A backswing on **Balenciaga** evening dresses, a bustle from **Dior**, silk jerseys from **Grès**, a high waist and satin ribbon from **Fath**, tulle and lace from **Balmain** and chiffon gowns from **Griffe** and **Desses** are a few highlights.

WHAT A YEAR IT WAS!

1953

Dresses are...

slim, patterned and pink for summer evenings.

New trends include dresses without belts, shorter coats for day, longer coats for night, long and thin purses, black stockings, herringbone dresses, low necklines, animal prints and the color **red.**

Suits are...
three pieces—the skirt, the jacket and the blouse.

Patterns such as paisley are seen on blouses and the chic, close-to-the-head silk turbans. Be sure to accompany your turban with big earrings.

HERE COMES THE BRIDE

ANKLE-, BALLERINA- OR COCKTAIL-LENGTH GOWNS MADE OF LINEN, EMBROIDERED COTTON OR CHIFFON WITH JEWELED HEADPIECES AND MEDIUM-LENGTH VEILS MAKE 1953'S BRIDE THE PICTURE OF PERFECTION.

THE COLORS

GRAY, YELLOW, BLUE, RED, BLACK *and all shades of* BROWN, *including* CHESTNUT, TAUPE, BEIGE, PECAN *and* BRONZE.

THE FABRICS

SATIN, PIQUÉ, CASHMERE, COTTON, JERSEY, LINEN, SILK, LACE, ORGANDY, CHIFFON, FLEECE, WOOL *and* VELVET.

1953

The **"New in Shoes"** promotion, designed to boost sales for the shoe industry, is launched by the National Shoe Institute with a spring and fall showing of the latest footwear.

Casual shoes for women, in a variety of styles, remain all the rage for sportswear. **Moccasins, pumps, flats, mules** and the **Spanish toe** are fashionable.

Black shoes gain popularity for men, while **navy** and **red** are trendy for kids.

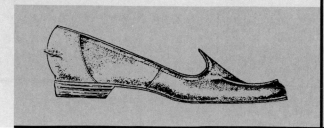

WHAT A YEAR IT WAS!

Pink gloves

any which way—
cotton, handmade,
seersucker, linen,
patterned,
embroidered,
buttoned, appliquéd,
cuffed—make
any outfit a
bit snappier.

bella donna

The hairstyle of the year is the new Italian cut — short with curls near the ears worn with large hoop earrings.

1953

Just A Little TUG *Over Here*

Look slender after you squeeze yourself into the newest foundation—all-in-one from your shoulders to your thighs in black.

"Everything's Rosy" is Revlon's newest super-pink lipstick and nail polish while the latest red lipstick from Max Factor Hollywood is "Riding Hood Red."

1953

THE BEST-DRESSED WOMEN IN THE WORLD

Mrs. Louis Arpels

Mrs. Henry Ford II

Mrs. Winston Guest

Mrs. William Randolph Hearst, Jr.

Oveta Culp Hobby

Princess Margaret

Mary Martin

Barbara "Babe" Paley

Mrs. Alfred G. Vanderbilt

Duchess of Windsor

Princess Margaret

PASSINGS

Edwin Goodman
76

Guccio Gucci
71

Carrie Marcus Neiman
69

WHAT A YEAR IT WAS!

New PRODUCTS & INVENTIONS

1953

Is it... SMALLER *Than* A BREADBOX?

NBC introduces the smallest television film camera tube ever developed for broadcast use.

PROGRAM SPONSORS WILL LOVE THIS

A new 3-dimensional TV process called "*Genoscope*," which requires special eyeglasses to be worn by the viewer, is demonstrated by the inventor, Mrs. Genevieve Lott-Fuller, wife of 3-D movie inventor Edgar Fuller.

BELL TELEPHONE

Laboratories creates "Audrey," a new electronic telephone with a programmable memory capacity thought to be a major step toward eliminating the need to dial a number.

IBM unveils the "701," a high-speed electronic calculator.

A new surveillance radar system that tracks the location and flight path of all aircraft flights within 30 to 60 miles of the airport is unveiled by **General Electric** and placed in operation at a municipal airport.

Paul R. Forgrave of Washington, D.C. applies for a patent on his new invention—combination 3-D glasses and sunglasses.

You Gotta Have HEART

Devised by two Detroit doctors, a new mechanical heart is credited with saving four lives.

1953

How Sweet It Is
The commercial food packaging industry is introduced to a process that dehydrates sweet corn.

No Need To Spit Out The Pits

Chemists of the Bureau of Agricultural and Industrial Chemistry introduce a new orange juice powder with the color, flavor and nutritional content of fresh orange juice.

Just Add Ice Cubes And Voilà, Instant Chemical Mix

The world's first instant iced tea, White Rose "Redi-Tea," is brought to the market by New York's Seeman Brothers.

FROZEN BREAD
is available through Arnold Bakers, Inc., of Port Chester, N.Y. to consumers in many parts of the U.S.

AND NOW INTRODUCING A FOODLESS WONDER
"Kraft Cheez Whiz" starts appearing on crackers around the country.

GOING FOR A HIGHER "C"

A new superior tomato named "Doublerich," which contains two times as much vitamin C as standard varieties, has been developed jointly by the North Dakota and New Hampshire agricultural experiment stations.

PRESTO!
A PICTURE OF YOUR SMILING DOG

Edwin H. Land, inventor of the Polaroid "one-minute" Land Camera, comes up with new color film offering instant color prints.

Put Away Those Waffle Irons And Pass The Syrup
Toasters are popping up the new "Eggo" frozen waffles for the first time.

Armour Research Foundation of the Illinois Institute of Technology invents "Chem-Dry," a process for rapid drying of protective and decorative coatings of inks, paints and varnishes.

Minneapolis-Honeywell Regulator Co. develops new electronic equipment that regulates indoor temperatures automatically.

SAFE ENOUGH FOR BABY TO "EAT"
Sapolin Paints comes out with a quick-drying, lead-free enamel paint specifically for use on children's toys and furniture.

SOMETHING TO GET ALL CLINGY ABOUT
"Saran Wrap" becomes the first plastic wrap targeted for home use.

SPRAY ON – WIPE OFF
A new aerosol glass cleaner called "Spray-Away" hits the market.

THE DUST BITES THE DUST
"Endust," a dusting aid in an aerosol can, helps housewives clean up those dust balls more efficiently.

And from Holland, Michigan, **Raymond H. Ryzenga** brings us a doormat with built-in brushes that knock the dirt off the soles of your shoes.

Yummies For Your Favorite Rhododendron
A new plant food developed by DuPont called "Soluble Plant Food" offers a balanced diet for plants.

ICE
ON COMMAND
Ice cubes made without trays are now available through a completely automatic ice-maker introduced by Servel, Inc. of Evansville, Indiana.

If You Can't Take The Heat, Use This
Pyrene Mfg. Co. of Newark, N.J. introduces an all-purpose fire extinguisher to use on small fires.

NO MORE SHORT FUSES
The screw-in fuse is being replaced by a circuit breaker called the "Mini-Breaker," manufactured by Mechanical Products, Inc. of Jackson, Michigan.

1953

DICK TRACY LIVES

A new wrist radio and pocket transmitter has been developed by the Signal Corps Engineering Laboratories in Fort Monmouth, New Jersey.

To protect against flying metal particles from high-speed milling and cutting equipment, employees of **Lockheed Aircraft Corp.** in Burbank, California are wearing bulletproof aprons weighing less than 3 pounds.

NO MORE RAIN-DROPS FALLING ON YOUR HEAD

"*Weather-Guard*," a device which automatically raises convertible tops and windows at the first drop of rain, is being manufactured by a company based in New York and Miami.

The Graphic Arts

Research Foundation perfects a new type-composing machine called the "Photon," which completely eliminates the use of conventional lead type resulting in sharper printing.

JUST A LITTLE DAB WILL PROTECT YA

The "Shield," an invisible water repellent for fabrics and garments, is unveiled by the Surface Protection Co., Cleveland, Ohio.

SO, YOU WANNA BE ASLEEP AT THE WHEEL?
RCA develops the forerunner of a car with automatic steering, administered by an electronic robot.

BUCKLE UP FOR SAFETY
Similar to airplane safety belts, the "Karbelt" is introduced for use in both front and back seats.

> The new CHEVROLET CORVETTE becomes the first car produced to have an all-fiberglass body.
>
> •
>
> The first production Corvette rolls off the assembly line.

SHAVE 'N' DRIVE
Complete with an adaptor for use in the car lighter socket, the first battery-operated electric shaver is offered to consumers by North American Philips Co., Inc. of New York.

130

WHAT A YEAR IT WAS!

ATTENTION OFFICE WORKERS: YOU MAY NOW WASH YOUR HANDS AT YOUR DESK

Secretaries, stenographers and clerks no longer have to leave their desks to wash their hands thanks to a new product called "Steno-Crème," a water-less cleanser fortified with lanolin for removing ink, carbon and typewriter ribbon smudges.

The "Flexowriter," a new tape-operated electric typewriter with a memory capable of storing information, retrieves data, thus eliminating the need to retype the same information again.

Bombs Away In Baby's Bath

New York's **Ideal Toy Company** launches a toy submarine that floats just beneath the water's surface in junior's bathtub equipped with two torpedoes that can be fired from tubes on either side of its hull.

JAPAN IS LISTENING

Prerecorded videotapes for home use are thought to have future consumer market potential after recorder-playback units become more affordable. Current cost: around $60,000.

BLOWING IN THE WIND
A Midwestern tornado is recorded for the first time by a radar movie camera.

A CLOSER LOOK AT THOSE GAMS

A lighter-weight nylon hosiery yarn developed by DuPont will soon be available to women under the brand name "ultra sheer."

THIS SHOULD MAKE YOU LIGHTER ON YOUR FOOT
The Econ-O-Lite Company of Denver, Colorado puts out a simple device in the form of a light warning motorists when they are wasting gas by over-accelerating.

One of the newest materials developed by DuPont is "Mylar," a synthetic film that looks like cellophane but is much tougher and resistant to temperature and humidity changes.

How this "trick" can save you battery trouble

We don't recommend frying eggs on the hood of a car, but it does demonstrate what kills most batteries. Scorching underhood temperatures—heat from hard summer driving and overcharging generators— "bake out" a battery's starting punch. But the damage doesn't show up until the first cold spell.

On cold mornings you need *extra* power to kick over your engine. And a "baked out" battery just doesn't have it.

Have an Atlas dealer test your battery today. A 6-point variation in reading between cells indicates you need a new battery.

ATLAS
TIRES · BATTERIES
ACCESSORIES

An Atlas "H.D." battery supplies plenty of punch to meet the demands of modern automobiles for increased electrical power.

You'll get a written warranty on your new Atlas battery. It's honored by 38,000 Atlas dealers in 48 states and Canada.

See *your* Atlas dealer today. Be safe with an Atlas "H.D." battery. It gives 31.1% better zero starting power than S.A.E.† standards.

†Society of Automotive Engineers

38,000 ATLAS DEALERS SERVING MOTORISTS EVERYWHERE

*TRADE-MARK REG. COPYRIGHT 1953, ATLAS SUPPLY COMPANY, NEWARK 2, N. J.

SCIENCE 1953

AMAMAZON ANNIE WEAPON

The U.S. Army unveils **Amazon Annie**, a mobile cannon that fires both conventional high explosives and atomic artillery shells.

A battalion of these potent weapons is being shipped to Europe in support of NATO forces.

The U.S. Defense Department releases the first films of **Amazon Annie** actually firing an atomic shell.

With its recognizable atomic cloud, these blasts are the most lethal ever unleashed by any artillery weapon in history.

WHAT A YEAR IT WAS!

NOBEL PRIZES

PHYSIOLOGY or MEDICINE
Sir Hans A. Krebs
(Great Britain)
Fritz A. Lipmann
(USA)

PHYSICS
Frits (Frederik) Zernike
(The Netherlands)

CHEMISTRY
Hermann Staudinger
(Germany)

Einstein...

MR. SMARTY PANTS

Dr. Albert Einstein publishes in the Princeton University Press a group of formulas to describe mathematically the laws by which the universe operates.

Einstein announces revision of his theory of gravitation and that the improved theory sets forth in equations, understandable only to those familiar with higher geometries, that light, magnetism, radiation and gravitation are a unity and part of one "continuum."

SOLVING THE RIDDLE

Indiana University mathematician and Czech refugee, Professor **Vaclav Hlavaty**, claims that he has solved Einstein's "unified field" equation and that the theory might now be submitted for experimental verification.

WHAT A YEAR IT WAS!

atomic NEWS 1953

OATMEAL WITH A DASH OF GAMMA

The Atomic Energy Commission reveals an experiment in which oats are made immune to rust by being exposed to radiation from an atomic pile.

THAT AIN'T OATS

According to its semiannual report, the U.S. Atomic Energy Commission has invested $7,500,000,000 in nuclear research and development.

A HOT TIME IN THE OLD TOWN TONIGHT

In the first cancer therapy unit of its kind in the U.S., New York's Montefiore Hospital unveils the cobalt "bomb," reported to produce gamma rays with energy equal to all the medically used radium in the world.

A HEADY EXPERIENCE

With over 100 scientists from 19 countries in attendance, the first International Conference on Atomic Power for Industrial Uses is held in Oslo, Norway and adopts a resolution promoting peaceful use of nuclear power through international exchange of nonmilitary information.

Lighting UP THE SKIES

Eleven atomic explosions in 80 days are staged by the U.S. Atomic Energy Commission at the Nevada proving grounds, the tenth being the firing of the first atomic artillery shell in the history of the world.

AND IT ISN'T EVEN JULY 4TH

A-bomb test, twice as powerful as the bombs used in Japan, lights up the Nevada desert skies.

THE RUSSIANS REVEAL THAT THEY HAVE MASTERED THE SECRET OF THE H-BOMB.

Complete with stainless steel vaults for storing radioisotopes, Chicago's Argonne Cancer Research Hospital, built by the U.S. Atomic Energy Commission, is the world's first atomic hospital dedicated to the diagnosis and treatment of cancer and allied diseases.

WHAT A YEAR IT WAS!

FLYING HIGH

The YF-100A Super Sabre, the first combat aircraft capable of sustained supersonic-level flight, is tested by the U.S.

In a test, a radio-guided Navy AD-2 Skyraider plane is hurled to earth as it attempts the first flight through the center of a nuclear explosion.

Said to be the fastest speed ever attained by an aircraft, U.S. Air Force Major Charles E. Yeager, piloting a Bell X-1A rocket-powered plane, flies at a speed of more than 1,600 mph.

THEY CAN FLY, BUT THEY CAN'T HIDE

U.S. Army unveils a new rapid-firing radar-controlled anti-aircraft gun designed to search out hostile aircraft in all kinds of weather and to destroy them at altitudes of up to 4 miles.

The U.S. Army installs the nation's first battery of surface-to-air missiles, launching the era of guided weapons in warfare.

Look Ma, No Hands

In preparation for future interplanetary travel, the U.S. Air Force produces a no-gravity situation for jet pilots with no ill effects reported as a result of maintaining a weightless state for 42 seconds, other than a brief period of confusion.

THE NUKING REPORT

Operation of the Manhattan District and the Atomic Energy Commission over the last 10 years has resulted in two deaths and 19 cases of significant radiation injuries.

WHAT A YEAR IT WAS!

DOUBLING YOUR PLEASURE

Writing in the journal **Nature**, English scientists Rosalind Franklin and Francis Crick and American scientist James Watson discover the double-helical structure of DNA, making it possible to envisage how genes replicate and carry information.

Too Old To Have A Son?

An extensive study reveals that the age of the father and not the age of the mother affects the human sex ratio, with older fathers having relatively fewer sons.

Are You My Daddy?

University of Iowa scientists report the first pregnancies using deep-frozen sperm inseminated artificially.

The Argonne National Laboratory of the Atomic Energy Commission develops the **Oracle**, the fastest of all the electronic super-brains and the greatest memory capacity of any high-speed computer ever built.

FASTER THAN A SPEEDING COMPUTER

Massachusetts Institute of Technology's **Norbert Wiener**, expert on electronic brains, concludes that these devices lack the complexity of the human mind and that the number of switching devices in the human brain vastly exceed the number in any existing computing machine or one considered for future development.

WARNING

Better Hide The Matches

An article appearing in *The New York Times* states that pyromaniacs are the most difficult criminals to apprehend.

DIGGING
into the PAST

Tools dating back 500,000 years to the early Ice Age are discovered at Ain Hanech near St. Arnaud, Algeria.

A LITTLE PAINT
— It'll Be As Good As New

The remains of a 5,500-year-old Bronze Age village are uncovered in Israel's Negev Desert.

The Man Who Wasn't

The British Museum of Natural History reports that chemical tests reveal that the skull submitted by Charles Dawson in 1912 is not the skull of Piltdown Man but rather an elaborate and carefully prepared hoax.

> **New data released by a University of Texas professor indicates that America has been inhabited for well over 15,000 years.**

THAT'S A WHOLE LOT OF CANDLES

Using a chemical similar to the lead found in high-test gasoline to determine the age of the earth's crust, tests reveal the earth is 3,500,000,000 years old.

and it never, ever DEGRADES

German chemist Karl Ziegler invents a new catalytic process for polyethylene.

Whoops,
So That's Where You've Been, You Little Devil

A deadly virus discovered alive and kicking after 35 years in a test tube at the University of Michigan may bring about a major revision in scientific thought in the field of bacteriology.

GET OUT THOSE BOOTS AND UMBRELLAS

Using radar in weather forecasting warns New Yorkers of an approaching severe thunderstorm, which is being tracked from eastern Pennsylvania and New Jersey.

A survey conducted by the Los Alamos Scientific Laboratory on salaries paid to professional scientists and engineers shows that a Ph.D. degree is worth about $40,000 in additional salary over the course of one's career.

DADDY, WHY IS THE SKY BLUE?

One of the nation's top scientific educators, Joel H. Hildebrand of the University of California, says answering your child's questions as early as preschool could increase his chances of following a scientific career.

A cosmic ray observatory is erected on Mt. Wrangell, Alaska.

VITAMINS BE GONE

An article appearing in the Journal of Agricultural and Food Chemistry *indicates that irradiation of milk and other dairy products with gamma rays causes severe loss in the nutritional content.*

IS THERE LIFE AFTER EARTH?

Soviet astronomer G. A. Tikhov reports that he has discovered life on Mars in the form of blue and violet vegetation.

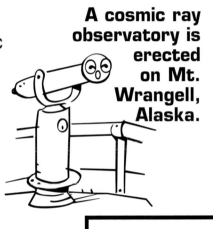

ROOM FOR EXPANSION

Using the 200-inch Mt. Palomar telescope, Dr. Edwin Hubble of Mt. Wilson Observatory in Pasadena, California supports the theory that the universe is expanding.

PASSING

EDWIN POWELL HUBBLE (63)

KOHLER
PLUMBING FIXTURES
first quality and value

When you build or remodel, you can afford Kohler quality in fixtures and fittings. They are made in a wide range of styles and sizes to meet any space or budget requirement. All bear the Kohler mark of first quality and value, and provide the true economy of long satisfactory service.

Kohler fixtures are as convenient as they are beautiful—and easy to clean. The Cosmopolitan Bench Bath has a low front, flat, roomy bottom, slope end, mixer fitting. The Hampton lavatory has a handy shelf, integral soap dishes, generous basin. Both are of enameled, non-flexing iron, cast for strength and rigidity. The chromium-plated fittings match in style and quality.

Consult your Kohler dealer when planning a bathroom, washroom, kitchen or laundry. Write for folder F-15.

Kohler Co., Kohler, Wisconsin. Established 1873

KOHLER OF KOHLER

PLUMBING FIXTURES · HEATING EQUIPMENT · ELECTRIC PLANTS · AIR-COOLED ENGINES · PRECISION CONTROLS

Medicine

38-year-old **DR. JONAS E. SALK** announces that the development of new vaccines against poliomyelitis has advanced to the point where they can be tested through mass inoculation of children.

The University of Miami reports that a few people have recovered from polio after they were injected with a preparation made from cobra venom.

The development of a new antibiotic called tetracycline is reported in the *Journal of the American Chemical Society.*

Saving The T-BONE

Instead of taking a steak out of the fridge if someone comes home with a black eye, Dr. Franklin M. Foote of the National Society for the Prevention of Blindness says using cold compresses for 20 to 30 minutes every three hours will reduce swelling and bruising.

Ouchless INJECTIONS

By incorporating a small, automatic refrigeration unit in hypodermic equipment, Dr. H. L. Mueller of Boston's Children's Hospital has invented a painless injection.

Typhoid vaccine has been successfully used by two Pasadena, California physicians in treating encephalitis or "sleeping sickness."

A study conducted by Dr. Jonas E. Salk indicates that immunization with a newly developed flu vaccine could last for at least two years.

Scientific director of New York's Memorial Center for Cancer & Allied Diseases, Dr. Cornelius P. Rhodes, expresses optimism that a cancer-curing drug will be found by 1963.

1953

Get Out That Baby Jungle Gym

The three things a growing child needs are food, sleep and exercise, with parents often paying very little attention to the last.

STRIKE WHILE THE IRON'S HOT

Your run-of-the-mill thermometer is being used as an indicator of a woman's fertile and nonfertile periods, helping many women to become pregnant.

Less Work For Mother

An article appearing in the *Southern Medical Journal* outlines a new concept of baby feeding which puts the infant on a schedule of three meals a day and calls for the introduction of foods other than milk as early as the second day of life.

Today's Health reports that due to the advances of modern medicine, nine out of ten premature babies have a good chance of surviving.

LOOKING UP TO YOUR CHILDREN

Today's children are taller on average than their parents and grandparents.

An expectant mother's physical and emotional health appear to have a direct bearing on giving birth to a normal or neurotic child, according to Dr. William S. Kroger of the Chicago Medical School.

The first synthesizing of a pituitary hormone, oxytocin, a uterine-contracting and milk-releasing agent, is reported by Dr. Vincent du Vigneaud, head of a Cornell University research team.

Test Tube Babies

About 10,000 American children under the age of 15 are the result of artificial insemination.

*A*n article appearing in *Nature*, British journal of science, reports successful artificial insemination at the University of Iowa Medical School with semen preserved by freezing.

WHAT A YEAR IT WAS!

Thinking

Citing the fact that alcohol does not dissolve in fatty tissue, Dr. Grace Eggleton of London's University College concludes that alcohol is likely to have a greater effect on stout people than on thin people, thereby making them more dangerous if they drive after drinking.

Something To Be Said For Cream Soda "COCKTAILS"

Young people tend to drink if their parents do, according to a study conducted at Yale University.

Stay Away From Those Twinkies

The Nutrition Foundation reports that Americans, the best-fed population in the world, are suffering from nutritional imbalance, adding that if one must drink alcohol, it should be followed by eating meat, potatoes and green vegetables.

University of Chicago sleep expert Dr. Nathaniel Kleitman asserts that seven hours of sleep is sufficient to maintain health and well-being and that it should be possible for the average adult to remain awake for 17 out of 24 hours without fatigue.

COULD BE INJURIOUS TO YOUR HEALTH

Speaking before the Midwestern Psychological Association, Dr. Edmund Jacobson asserts that thinking can make you as tired as hard labor and can result in high blood pressure, coronary heart disease and peptic ulcers. He describes a new method of teaching patients to relax by having them monitor their reactions on a television screen.

Yuk It Up And Live Longer

The Illinois State Medical Society advises that laughing is a good tonic as it brings about relaxation, which eases the strain on the heart, stimulates the adrenal glands to excrete more fluid, ventilates the lung spaces and exercises glands located in the neck and throat.

If carried out consistently and in moderation, exercise is an important aid in losing weight, according to doctors at the Harvard School of Public Health.

You Botcha Me, I Botcha You

After conducting tests on male volunteers, bacteriologist Arthur B. Bryan concludes that kissing "can be not only a pleasant but harmless pastime if ordinary lip and oral hygiene are practiced."

THE MAGIC BULLET

One shot of Bicillin, a long-acting penicillin, has proven safe and effective for curing primary and secondary syphilis, which has afflicted two million Americans.

REMOVING HAIRS FROM YOUR CHINNEY, CHIN, CHIN

BEFORE

AFTER

According to a cosmetic authority for the American Medical Association the only safe way you can permanently remove excess hair from the face or body is by electrolysis — electrical destruction of the root.

CO_2 CO_2

CO_2

An article appearing in the *New England Journal of Medicine* says that blowing into a paper bag and then inhaling the exhaled air is an effective treatment for dizziness and weakness resulting from lack of oxygen in the brain and is a quick fix for patients with arteriosclerosis and high blood pressure.

Dr. J. L. Richardson reports in the *Georgia Medical Association Journal* that there does not appear to be a correlation between attacks of coronary thrombosis and exercise, concluding that such heart attacks can occur at any time and are not related to the person's activity or emotional state.

Dr. James R. Gay, of White Plains, New York, reports that modern traffic conditions are producing many minor collisions which may result in persistent neck injuries.

RELIEVING THOSE STIFF JOINTS

An article appearing in the *Archives of Internal Medicine* reveals that placental blood serum has been effective in treating rheumatoid arthritis.

Mahatma Gandhi used this herb in a crude form to overcome his nervousness and insomnia and now Dr. Robert W. Wilkins of Boston University is using the same compound, known as **Rauwolfia serpentina**, in successfully treating milder forms of high blood pressure in young people.

1953

THAT'S A LOT OF BASKET WEAVING

National Association for Mental Health reports there are 650,000 patients in U.S. mental hospitals and that 20-25% of American workers are affected by mental and emotional disturbances.

A Yale University psychiatrist concludes that Americans are not any more neurotic than citizens of other countries, adding that with America's high standard of living and good health care, they are more introspective and concerned with their relationships with others.

DON'T REACH FOR A KLEENEX – REACH FOR A SHRINK

A stuffed or runny nose may be caused by emotional upset rather than a common cold, according to a doctor at the University of Oklahoma School of Medicine.

I WILL SLEEP, I Will Sleep, I Will Sleep, I WILL SLEEP

Danish psychiatrist Dr. Gudmund Magnussen says that the fear of not being able to sleep is one of the most common causes of insomnia.

You Gotta Accentuate The Positive

In what he terms as "hypochondrial distress," Dr. Herbert Ratner, health commissioner of Oak Park, Illinois, says that people

should spend less time being preoccupied with disease and death and should put limits on self-medication and spend more time promoting positive health.

SPELLING OUT THE SPELL

The JOURNAL OF THE AMERICAN MEDICAL ASSOCIATION says that the chill up and down your spine is not caused by black magic but is due to secretion of adrenaline and is a remnant of the primitive response of the erection of hair.

GAMMA GLOBULIN is used extensively throughout the U.S. during the summer months for prevention of poliomyelitis.

How Long Did You Say I Have To Wait For An Appointment?

According to the American Dental Association, there are 84,215 dentists in the U.S., or one for every 1,691 people.

Average per patient daily hospital cost:

$19.55

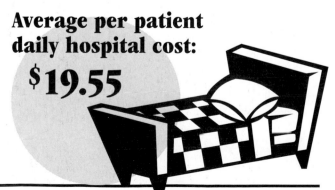

AMERICAN MAKES HISTORY WITH THE

First NONSTOP service
– coast to coast!

Now-Transcontinental Travel
UNDER 8 HOURS
on the New DC-7 Flagship

AMERICAN AIRLINES INC.
America's Leading Airline

In introducing the new DC-7 Flagship, American Airlines again demonstrates its leadership in air transportation with the first *nonstop* coast-to-coast service. For the first time in history—and at no extra fare—travelers will span the nation in less than eight hours.

Highlighting the many new developments in this magnificent Flagship are the special soundproofing that makes it the quietest plane aloft, the new 3350 horsepower "Turbo Compound" engines, and an air conditioning system that operates on the ground as well as in the air.

Beginning November 29th, there will be two round-trip DC-7 *nonstop* flights daily at regular Flagship fares. Make your reservation with American Airlines now. Be among the first travelers in history to enjoy coast-to-coast service *nonstop*.

146

BUSINESS — 1953

American car companies make over six million autos.

A record 63,408,000 Americans are employed in August. During the same time unemployment reaches its lowest figure since World War II – 1,240,000, which is 1.9% of the workforce. The typical workweek is 40 1/2 hours.

I AM WOMAN, HEAR ME ROAR

Atlanta architect June Wicker is chosen American Businesswoman of the Year.

STOP

Ladies become school crossing guards in Philadelphia for the first time.

The Gross National Product is approximately $368 billion.

A record $26 billion is held in U.S. savings banks.

The national debt is over $266 billion.

Bonds offering 3 1/4 % interest are released by the Department of the Treasury.

The Small Business Administration is established.

Interest rates are raised to 4 1/2 %.

The **New York Curb Exchange** becomes the **American Stock Exchange**.

Hotels Statler is chosen best-managed business in America by the American Institute of Management.

Don Corleone, I Presume

Hilton Hotels International agrees to manage the Havana Hilton, which will be owned and constructed by the Hotel & Restaurant Workers Federation, a Cuban union.

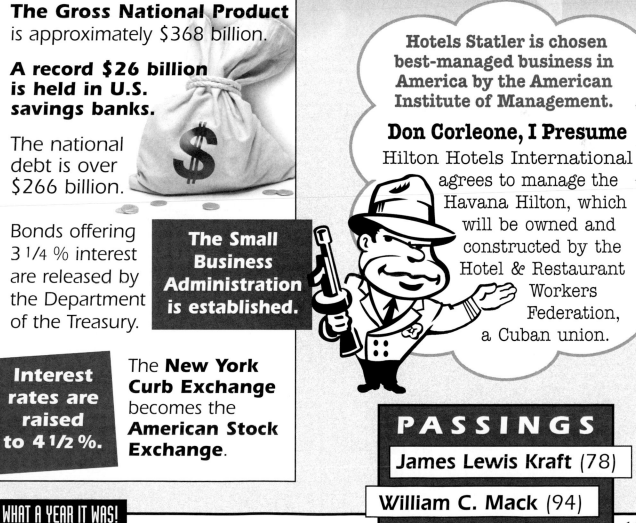

PASSINGS

James Lewis Kraft (78)

William C. Mack (94)

According to National Business & Property Exchange in Los Angeles, people who want to start their own businesses usually are interested in gas stations, hardware stores, motels, ranches, farms, commercial property, bars, five-and-dime stores, resorts and grocery stores.

A Little Artery-Clogging Cholesterol With My Fries, Please

The second McDonald's opens in Phoenix, Arizona, the third in North Hollywood, California and the fourth in Downey, California. The Phoenix restaurant is the first McDonald's to feature the golden arches.

Water & Cookies For The Young'Uns

Dairy farmers are forced to throw away good milk when New York drivers and milk handlers strike.

Si, Yo Tengo Un Biberon

Evenflo baby products opens a manufacturing plant in Mexico.

Americans spend roughly $1 billion on toys.

Over 10 million union members belong to the AFL.

CIO United Brewery Workers strike against Miller, Pabst, Schlitz and other brewers in the Milwaukee area. The strikers win raises ranging from 20¢-30¢ an hour in addition to a pension and paid lunches.

President Eisenhower invokes the Taft-Hartley Act against striking longshoremen on the Atlantic Coast.

CIO United Steelworkers of America win an 8 1/2 ¢ per hour pay raise from U.S. Steel Corp.

John L. Lewis is reelected president of the United Mine Workers, a position he has held since 1920.

Walter Reuther is reelected president of the United Auto Workers for the 5th time.

Of the 3.5 million black men working in the U.S., approximately 1.5 million are thought to be union members.

The 26,000-member Newspaper Guild holds its 20th convention.

The AFL expels the International Longshoremen's Association for racketeering.

AN UN-EN-LIGHT-ENED VIEW
General Electric declares it will fire any employee who confesses to being a Communist.

700 STRIKES ARE IN PROGRESS IN JULY.

A strike by three of France's biggest labor unions nearly paralyzes the country. Several of the affected industries include communications, railroads, mines and hospitals as well as the government.

STRIKE

UNFAIR!

WHAT A YEAR IT WAS!

This Is THE PRICE THAT WAS

FOOD BASKET

Apple Pie	$ .49
Bananas (lb.)	.15
Beets (bunch)	.07
Blueberries (lb.)	.29
Bread (loaf)	.15
Cabbage (lb.)	.05
Cake Mix	.29
Cantaloupe (lb.)	.09
Celery (stalk)	.15
Cheddar Cheese (lb.)	.49
Coffee (lb.)	.85
Crackers	.31
Ice Cream Cone	.07
Juice	.23

Ketchup	$ .21
Lettuce (head)	.05
Mayonnaise (qt.)	.53
Milk (qt.)	.22
Olive Oil	.55
Oranges (lb.)	.12
Peanut Butter	.43
Plums (lb.)	.23

HOME SWEET HOME
3-Bedroom House

Bucks County, PA	$ 17,000
Great Neck, NY	29,500
Rego Park, NY	14,750
Santa Monica, CA	15,500
Stamford, CT	24,500

YEARLY SALARIES

Accountant	$ 6,000
Architect	7,800
Attorney	7,500
Bank Teller	3,500
Chemist	6,500
Construction Worker	4,100
Copywriter	7,000
Engineer	8,500
Insurance Agent	6,000
Messenger	2,600
President Eisenhower	100,000
Secretary	3,900
State University Professor (STARTING SALARY)	5,525

1953

A LITTLE OF THIS...

Arthur Murray Dance Studio (LIFE MEMBERSHIP)	$8,000.00
Blanket	17.98
Borax	.18
Bulova Watch	57.50
Cloth Diapers (6)	.96
Coffeemaker	37.50
Cold Cream	1.25
Cough Syrup	.49
Crib	44.69
DDT Insect Bomb	1.39
Electric Food Mixer	59.50
Fan	29.95
Girdle	4.98
Iron	6.98
Kitchen Towel	.49

...A LITTLE OF THAT

Laundry Detergent	$ .33
Lincoln Logs	4.00
Men's Suit	59.50
Parakeet	5.75
Phonograph	152.95
Pillow	7.95
Sleeping Bag	16.88
Sofa	395.00
Television (17")	149.95
Toaster	26.50
Toothpaste	.59
Vitamins	1.75
Waffle Iron	9.95
Women's Robe	19.95

STOCKS

Alaska Airlines	4
Cessna Aircraft	7
JC Penney	69
Kaiser Motors	3 1/8
Motorola	38 5/8
Northrop	15
Parke-Davis	40
Pepsi-Cola	12
Pitney Bowes	20 1/2
Richfield Oil	60 1/2
RKO Pictures	3 1/2
Safeway Stores	36 7/8
Shell Oil	69 1/2
U.S. Steel	43 1/2
Walgreens	27 1/2

The average price of a share on the New York Stock Exchange is $46.56.

ON THE GO

Balsawood Raft	$ 29.88
Brake Adjustment	2.50
Car Rental, Daily Rate	9.00
Children's Bicycle	19.75
Ford Automobile	1,795.00
Tire	16.95
Train Set	26.77
Train, LA to Chicago	55.44

Toward the end of the year, Texas Instruments is listed on the New York Stock Exchange for the first time. Shares sell for $5.25.

WHAT A YEAR IT WAS!

Get rid of adhesive stamps and lick-and-stick mailing . . . The DM Postage Meter (desk model) *prints* postage for any kind of mail, directly on the envelope, with a small ad if you like. Has a moistener for sealing envelopes. Protects, and accounts for postage. Even handles parcel post. Models for larger offices. Ask for demonstration.

Do away with tedious and costly hand folding. The FH Folding Machine makes eight basic folds, double-folds up to 5,000 sheets an hour! . . . Easy to set, can be used by anybody. Small, light, portable. Costs less than a typewriter! Pays for itself quickly. (Larger Model FM folds up to 19,000 per hour.) Ask for a demonstration.

Give everybody in your office a head start . . . open your morning mail easily, in a jiffy . . . with the PB MailOpener (electric LE). A guarded rotary blade takes any kind or size of envelope, fast as you can feed it. Three models. Ask for demonstration on your own mail, in your own office.

"You pay me too much—"

"Nice of you to mention it, Miss Allison."

"*Everybody* in this office is paid too much," she went on, "to waste time the way we do!"

"For instance?" said Mr. Jones, grinning.

"Well, folding the Bulletin ties us up every Wednesday afternoon. We sit around mornings until nine-thirty waiting for the mail to be opened. Getting out our mail runs into overtime too often. We still do too many things by hand that should be done by machine."

"I see," said Mr. Jones, *not* grinning.

Do *you* see how much time people in *your* office spend at repetitious small chores that could be better done by machine?

Good clerical workers are hard to find. Office salaries have moved up! Outmoded methods are as wasteful in the office as in the factory.

Mailing and other clerical jobs are speeded up and made easier in thousands of offices by Pitney-Bowes appliances. The postage meter, mailing scale, letter opener, and folding machine . . . all save time, cut costs in any office—*and particularly the small office.*

Ask the nearest Pitney-Bowes branch to show you! Or send coupon for free booklets.

FREE: *Handy wall chart of Postal Rates, with parcel post map and zone finder.*

PITNEY-BOWES Postage Meter

Made by the world's leading manufacturer of mailing machines . . . with offices in 93 cities in the United States and Canada.

PITNEY-BOWES, Inc.
2892 Pacific St.,
Stamford, Conn.

Send booklet on ☐ *DM Postage Meter* ☐ *FH Folding Machine*
☐ *MailOpener* ☐ *Mailing Scales* ☐ *Send Postal Rate Chart*

Name..

Firm...

Address...

Save postage with a PB precision Mailing Scale. *Over*paid mail wastes money, *under*paid mail wastes good will! The pendulum mechanism is fast-acting, accurate. Easy-to-read chart and hairline indicator save time, eyes, and postage. Four models. Ask for a demonstration.

DISASTERS

FLOODING LEAVES PEOPLE HOMELESS...

**Three million in India.
One million in Japan.
300,000 in Hong Kong.
100,000 in the Netherlands.
25,000 in Louisiana.**

Storms off Europe's North Sea cause severe flooding and thousands of deaths. The worst floods to hit the Netherlands in over 500 years take the lives of nearly 1,800 people and cause roughly $263 million in damage. More than 500 die in Britain.

A typhoon kills approximately 1,000 people in Vietnam.

Over 1,000 people are killed when an earthquake hits Turkey.

In southern India over 400 people die during one week from sunstroke due to scorching temperatures.

WHAT A YEAR IT WAS!

FIRES

Waterfront fires

cause $12 million in damage in Oakland, California, $15 million in Wilmington, North Carolina and $2 million in Baltimore, Maryland.

A factory explosion *followed by a fire kills 35 people in Chicago, Illinois.*

15 firefighters die *in the line of duty in California's Mendocino National Forest.*

In São Paulo, Brazil *a dance-hall fire takes the lives of 70 people.*

BY AIR

129 U.S. military men die *near Tokyo in the worst airplane accident in the history of aviation.*

11 people are killed *in the first deadly crash of a commercial plane when a Canadian jet crashes upon takeoff in Karachi, Pakistan.*

by sea

133 people drown *when the ferry Princess Victoria sinks during a storm on the Irish Sea en route to Northern Ireland from Scotland.*

WHAT A YEAR IT WAS!

YANKEES beat DODGERS

WINNING THEIR FIFTH STRAIGHT WORLD SERIES CHAMPIONSHIP

Story continues on following pages

1953

YANKEES beat

GAME 2

Fans cram into Yankee Stadium.

All tied up in the 8th inning, **Mickey Mantle**, at bat, faces Dodger pitcher **Preacher Rowe**.

With **Hank Bauer** onboard, the "Oklahoma Kid" parks it in the left field seats, so it's two runs for the Yankees to give them a 2-0 lead.

The fans go wild.

YANKEES beat
GAME
EBBETS FIELD

3

With the score tied in the 8th, **Roy Campanella** steps in and his round tripper puts the Dodgers out front.

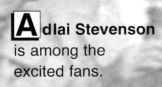

Adlai Stevenson is among the excited fans.

GAME 4

Snider hits another double. Hail the "Duke of Flatbush."

Duke Snider, Dodger center fielder, is the hero of this game. Snider's double to right in the first inning drives in two runs.

In the sixth inning the Duke hits one clear out of the park and there is new life and new hope in Brooklyn.

WHAT A YEAR IT WAS!

Campy comes home and the "Bums" tie up the series.

GAME 5

Mickey does it again. Another home run, only this time it's a grand slammer bringing home three teammates.

The fans go crazy.

An unhappy Dodger fan.

GAME 6

It's the top of the 9th and **Carl Furillo** blasts one to the opposite field and drops it in the right field corner for a home run. A dramatic moment, for with Snider on base, two runs come home for the Dodgers on Furillo's wallop. Now the score is tied at 3-3.

Yanks are now up and it's the bottom half of the 9th with Hank Bauer on second. **Billy Martin** is up and laces one right up the middle. His 12th hit of the series makes him the hero of heroes.

Bauer scores and the Yanks win the game 4-2 and the series, making baseball history. Five World Series in a row for **Casey Stengel** and his American League champions.

A jubilant Yankee fan.

BASEBALL ● NEWS

World Series
New York Yankees over Brooklyn Dodgers, 4-2

- Milwaukee gets its first baseball team since 1902 following unanimous approval by National League club owners to allow the Boston Braves franchise to relocate.

- American League club owners approve the transfer of the St. Louis franchise to Baltimore and the team is renamed the Orioles.

- Baseball's playing rules committee makes the following changes: a batter hitting a fly ball which permits a runner to score from third base is now credited with a sacrifice and not charged with an official time at bat.

The U.S. Supreme Court upholds the 1922 ruling by Associate Justice Oliver Wendell Holmes that professional baseball is a sport, not a business, and is not subject to federal antitrust laws.

⚾ Retired Philadelphia Athletics manager Connie Mack turns 91.

⚾ Brooklyn Dodger broadcaster since 1939, Walter "Red" Barber switches to the N.Y. Yankees.

⚾ New York's Yankee Stadium is sold by club owners Dan Topping and Del Webb to a Chicago group for $6,500,000.

⚾ The U.S. Supreme Court agrees to hear appeals contesting organized baseball's "reserve clause" contracts giving clubs complete control over players.

⚾ Still a long way from breaking Babe Ruth's record of 714, Ralph Kiner hits his 300th major league home run against New York but is still behind Yankees' Johnny Mize who has racked up 356 home runs. Mize makes his 2,000th major league hit in June as a pinch hitter against the St. Louis Browns, becoming the 93rd major leaguer to hit that number.

⚾ N.Y. Yankees pitcher Vic Raschi sets a major league record for pitchers by batting in seven runs against Detroit in Yankee Stadium.

⚾ St. Louis Cardinal 37-year-old Enos Slaughter gets his 2,000th major league hit.

⚾ Dizzy Dean and Al Simmons named to Baseball Hall of Fame in Cooperstown, New York.

LEO DUROCHER
signs up to continue as manager of the N.Y. Giants through the end of 1955 at an annual salary estimated to be between $50,000 to $60,000.

MICKEY MANTLE
N.Y. Yankee center fielder, 21-year-old Mickey Mantle, hits a home run in Washington that travels around 565 feet, becoming the first hit over the left field bleachers in Griffith Stadium.

Home Run Leaders
National League
Eddie Matthews (Milwaukee, 47)
American League
Al Rosen (Cleveland, 43)

Batting Champions
National League
Carl Furillo (Brooklyn, .344)
American League
Mickey Vernon (Washington, .337)

Most Valuable Player
National League
Roy Campanella (Brooklyn)
American League
Al Rosen (Cleveland)

Strikeouts
National League
Robin Roberts (Philadelphia, 198)
American League
Billy Pierce (Chicago, 186)

Rookie Of The Year
National League
Jim Gilliam (Brooklyn)
American League
Harvey Kuenn (Detroit)

All-Star Game
National over American, 5-1
(5 innings due to rain)
Casey Stengel, American Manager
Charlie Dressen, National Manager

WHAT A YEAR IT WAS!

Start your car shopping right here and end it at your Mercury dealer's

MERCURY'S POWER BRAKES WORK AS EASILY AS THE ACCELERATOR

POWER STEERING REDUCES TURNING EFFORT BY 75%

4-WAY POWER SEAT MOVES UP AND DOWN AS WELL AS BACK AND FORTH

COMPARE MERCURY AGAINST THE FIELD—AND ONLY A MERCURY WILL DO

Power steering, power brakes, 4-way power seat, white side-wall tires and full-disc hubcaps optional at extra cost.

Of course, we can only give you a brief preview here. When you stop at your Mercury dealer's showroom you'll get the full story—see for yourself how Mercury offers more for your money.

You'll get thrilling power and *proven* performance from that Mercury V-8 engine . . . the latest improvement in the only type of engine ever used in a Mercury!

You'll find long, low lines, with no "gingerbread" decorations, no bulges to look out of date in another year or two. You'll find colorful but practical interiors.

Best of all—you'll be buying economy. Save money on day-to-day operation—get back more money at trade-in time. So why not see your nearby Mercury dealer and start enjoying all this, and more—*today?*

Move ahead with **MERCURY** Get more for your money

Symbolizing the progress of Ford Motor Company's 50th Anniversary—"50 Years Forward on the American Road"

MERCURY DIVISION · FORD MOTOR COMPANY

FOOTBALL 1953

NATIONAL FOOTBALL LEAGUE CHAMPIONS

Detroit Lions over **Cleveland Browns**
17-16

MOST VALUABLE PLAYER

Otto Graham
Cleveland Browns, QB

NFL PRO BOWL

National
over **American**
27-7

NATIONAL COLLEGE FOOTBALL CHAMPIONS

Maryland

ROSE BOWL

USC over **Wisconsin**
7-0

HEISMAN TROPHY

Johnny Lattner
Notre Dame, HB

NEWS

Rules committee of the National Collegiate Athletic Association unanimously abolishes the free substitution rule in football, thereby ending the two-platoon system.

West Virginia to play against Georgia Tech in the Sugar Bowl.

Cornell wins Eastern (Ivy) League title.

Representing the Atlantic coast conference, Maryland is named to oppose Oklahoma, Big Seven champion, in the Orange Bowl.

OKLAHOMA DEFEATS IOWA STATE 47-0, winning its sixth straight Big Seven football conference title.

ARMY DEFEATS NAVY 20-7 for the first time since 1949, winning the Southwestern conference title.

Maryland football coach **James M. Tatum** is named **"coach of the year"** by U.S. football coaches.

PASSING

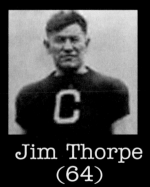

Jim Thorpe
(64)

EISENHOWER GREETS FAMOUS SPORTS FIGURES

43 top sports figures are the guests of President Eisenhower at the White House including Clark Griffith of baseball fame (*left of Ike*) and tennis star Lieutenant Commander Helen Jacobs.

Other champions represented are the one and only Joe DiMaggio (*left*) and golfer Gene Sarazin (*right of Lt. Commander Jacobs, above*).

Ike looks at Rocky Marciano's mighty hands and vetoes the idea of a match.

golf

U.S. OPEN	**Ben Hogan*** **Betsy Rawls**
PGA	**Walter Burkemo**
PGA/LPGA LEADING MONEY WINNER	**Lew Worsham** **$34,002** **Louise Suggs** **$16,892**
PGA PLAYER OF THE YEAR	**Ben Hogan**
MASTERS	**Ben Hogan***
U.S. AMATEUR	**Gene Littler** **Mary Lena Faulk**
BRITISH OPEN	**Ben Hogan***
SENIOR PGA	**Harry Schwab**

*Ben Hogan becomes the first golfer to win the Masters and the British and U.S. Open in a single year. He is also only one of three players to ever win the U.S. Open title four times.

WHAT A YEAR IT WAS!

The President and Mr. Jones

BOBBY JONES

The President and golf immortal Bobby Jones view the portrait painted by the Chief Executive of his favorite golfer in front of the trophy room of the famous Augusta Golf Course, which the President favors for his moments of leisure.

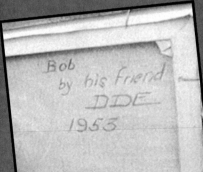

Bob
by his friend
DDE
1953

Ike presents his painting, which he copied from a photograph of Jones at his peak.

A self-critic, the President is not quite satisfied with the left eye, which he said was smudged. But to the Grand Slam winner, it's perfect!

1953 HORSE

WOOD
MEMORIAL
HORSE RACE

JAMAICA
GOLDEN JUBILEE
(1903-1953)

40,000 people turn out at **Jamaica** for this year's Wood Memorial, the richest race for three-year-olds ever run on the New York circuit.

The favorite is *Native Dancer* with **Eric Guerin** atop.

One dollar gets you ten cents if he wins and practically everybody here expects him to win this dress rehearsal for the Kentucky Derby.

WHAT A YEAR IT WAS!

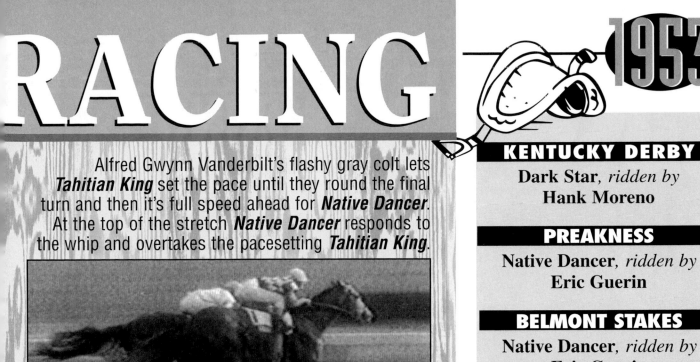

RACING

Alfred Gwynn Vanderbilt's flashy gray colt lets *Tahitian King* set the pace until they round the final turn and then it's full speed ahead for *Native Dancer*. At the top of the stretch *Native Dancer* responds to the whip and overtakes the pacesetting *Tahitian King*.

Even those rare railbirds who bet against him now view *Native Dancer* with admiration as he pounds down the stretch, opening the gap with every stride.

Native Dancer wins by four-and-a-half lengths his 11th race in as many starts, adding $87,000 to his fabulous earnings.

KENTUCKY DERBY
Dark Star, *ridden by*
Hank Moreno

PREAKNESS
Native Dancer, *ridden by*
Eric Guerin

BELMONT STAKES
Native Dancer, *ridden by*
Eric Guerin

HORSE OF THE YEAR
Tom Fool

MONEY LEADERS
Jockey **Willie Shoemaker**
$1,784,187
Horse **Native Dancer**
$513,425

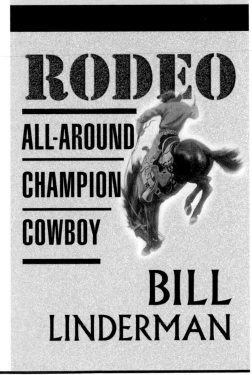

RODEO
ALL-AROUND
CHAMPION
COWBOY

BILL LINDERMAN

WHAT A YEAR IT WAS!

1953

BASKETBALL

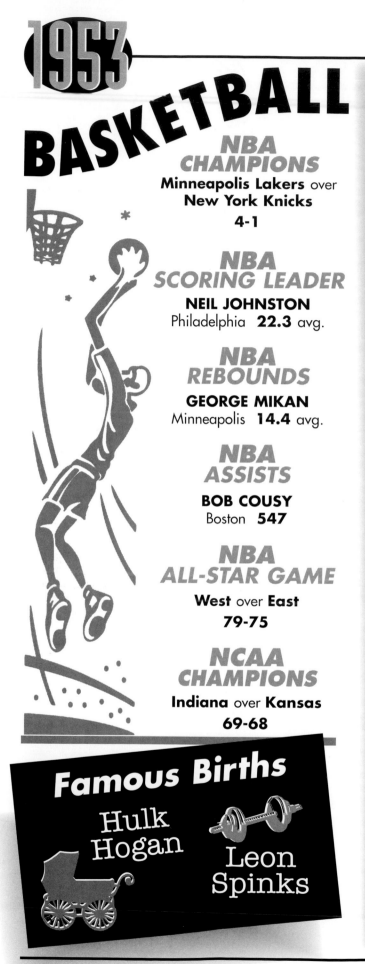

NBA CHAMPIONS
Minneapolis Lakers over
New York Knicks
4-1

NBA SCORING LEADER
NEIL JOHNSTON
Philadelphia **22.3** avg.

NBA REBOUNDS
GEORGE MIKAN
Minneapolis **14.4** avg.

NBA ASSISTS
BOB COUSY
Boston **547**

NBA ALL-STAR GAME
West over **East**
79-75

NCAA CHAMPIONS
Indiana over **Kansas**
69-68

Famous Births
Hulk Hogan
Leon Spinks

BOXING NEWS

Knocking out **Jersey Joe Walcott** in 2 minutes, 25 seconds, **Rocky Marciano** retains heavyweight title.

With 44,562 fans in attendance, the **Rocky Marciano-Roland LaStarza** world heavyweight championship bout garners the biggest gate of the year, pulling in $435,820. It is also the first nationwide theater telecast of a bout, bringing in another $125,000 in revenues.

A record 19 boxing deaths occur this year throughout the world, five of which are in the U.S.

HEAVYWEIGHT
ROCKY MARCIANO

MIDDLEWEIGHT
CARL "BOBO" OLSON

WELTERWEIGHT
KID GAVILAN

FEATHERWEIGHT
SANDY SADDLER

LIGHTWEIGHT
JAMES CARTER

LIGHT HEAVYWEIGHT
ARCHIE MOORE

170

WHAT A YEAR IT WAS!

1953

TENNIS

U.S. OPEN

TONY TRABERT over **VIC SEIXAS**

MAUREEN CONNOLLY* over **DORIS HART**

WIMBLEDON

VIC SEIXAS over **KURT NIELSEN**

MAUREEN CONNOLLY* over **DORIS HART**

DAVIS CUP

AUSTRALIA over **U.S., 3-2****

*18-year-old Connolly sets an all-time record for women's tennis, winning all four major singles championships in one year – the Australian, French, British and U.S.

**Ken Rosewall defeats Vic Seixas to take fourth straight Davis Cup for Australia.

TRACK & FIELD

BOSTON MARATHON

Keizo Yamada, Japan

TRACK & FIELD NEWS

Czech runner **EMIL ZATOPEK** sets world mark in 5,000 meters at 29:01.6.

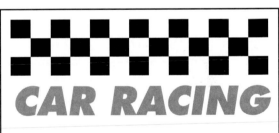

CAR RACING

INDIANAPOLIS 500

Bill Vukovich

Fuel Injection Special, 128.740 mph

LE MANS

Tony Rolt & Duncan Hamilton

Jaguar C, 98.65 mph

WINSTON CUP

Herb Thomas

1953

HOCKEY

STANLEY CUP CHAMPIONS

MONTREAL
CANADIENS
over
BOSTON
BRUINS
4-1

ROSS TROPHY
(LEADING SCORER)

GORDIE HOWE (Detroit)

VEZINA TROPHY
(OUTSTANDING GOALIE)

TERRY SAWCHUK (Detroit)

CALDER MEMORIAL TROPHY
(ROOKIE OF THE YEAR)

GUMP WORSLEY (New York)

LADY BYNG MEMORIAL TROPHY
(MOST GENTLEMANLY PLAYER)

RED KELLY (Detroit)

HART MEMORIAL TROPHY
(MVP)

GORDIE HOWE (Detroit)

CYCLING

TOUR de FRANCE
Louison Bobet
France

SWIMMING

EGYPT'S ABDEL LITIF ABOU HEIF swims the English Channel from England to France in a new record time of 13 hours, 45 minutes.

California's **FLORENCE CHADWICK**...

... sets English Channel swimming mark at 14 hours, 42 minutes.

... sets record swimming the Bosphorus Strait from Europe to Asia and back.

CHESS

WORLD CHAMPIONS
Mikhail Botvinnik (U.S.S.R.)
Ludmila Rudenko (U.S.S.R.)

U.S. CHAMPIONS
Larry Evans
Mary Bain

BILLIARDS

1953

WORLD POCKET BILLIARD CHAMPION
Willie Mosconi

Roller Derby
The **New Jersey Jolters** over **New York Chiefs**

BOWLING

BPAA ALL-STAR TOURNAMENT	**DON CARTER**
AMERICAN BOWLING CONGRESS	**FRANK SANTORE**
WOMEN'S INTERNATIONAL BOWLING CONGRESS	**DORIS KNECHTGES**
BOWLER OF THE YEAR	**DON CARTER** **MARION LADEWIG**

Figure Skating

U.S. & World Champions
- **Hayes Alan Jenkins**
- **Tenley Albright***

Pairs World Champions
- **John & Jennifer Nicks**

*17-year-old **Miss Albright** is the first American girl to win the championship, which followed her battle and recovery from polio*

ASSORTED AWARDS

AP ATHLETE OF THE YEAR
Ben Hogan (Golf)
Maureen Connolly (Tennis)

JAMES E. SULLIVAN MEMORIAL AWARD
Sammy Lee (Diving)

THE HICKOCK BELT
Ben Hogan (Golf)

1953 WAS A GREAT YEAR, BUT....

THE BEST IS YET TO COME!